CHURCH

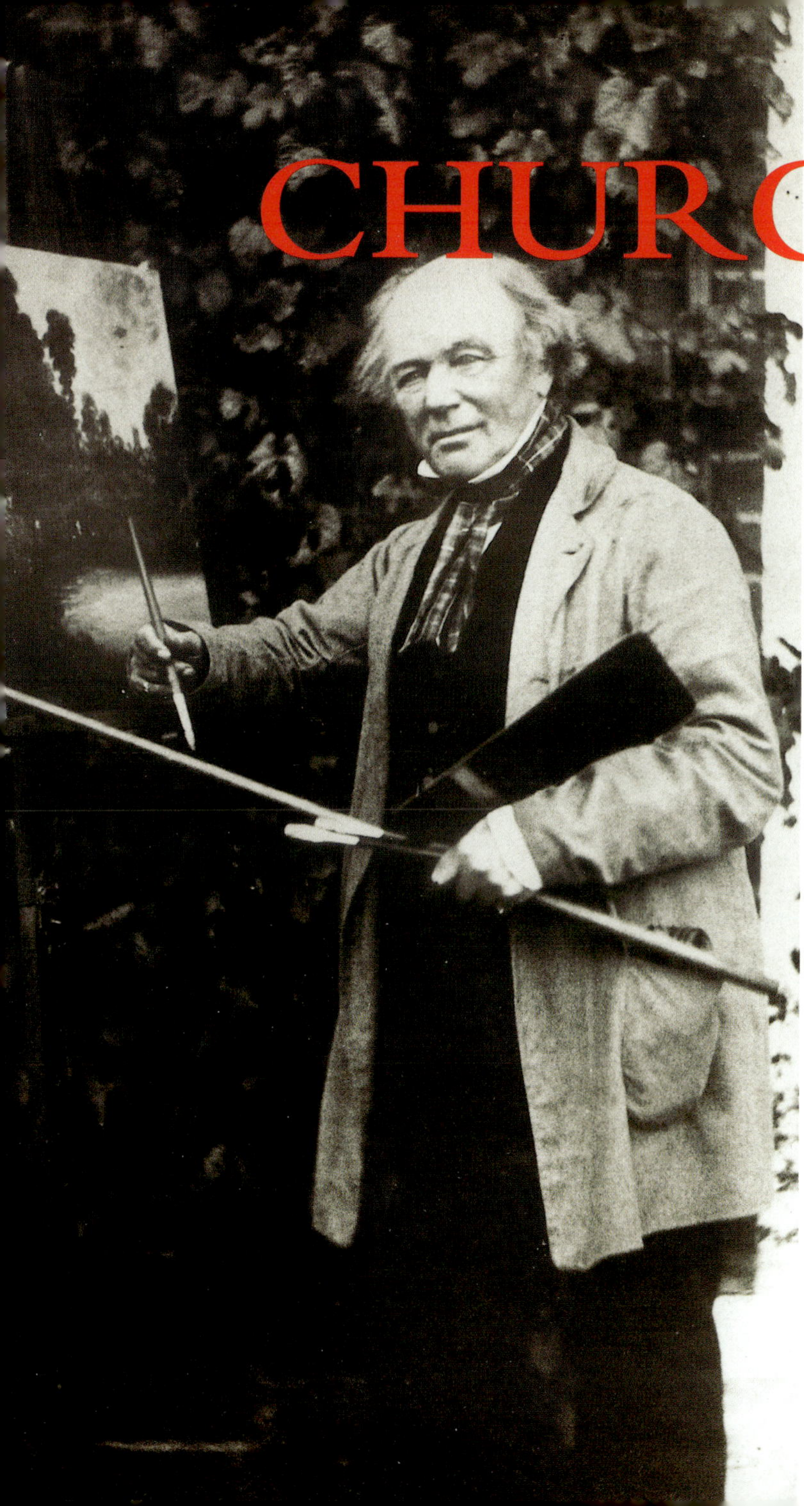

An Exhibition and
Sale of original works
to celebrate his
bicentenary

Research and text by
Stephen Reiss, O.B.E.

Reproduced by kind permission of Ipswich Borough Council Museums and Galleries

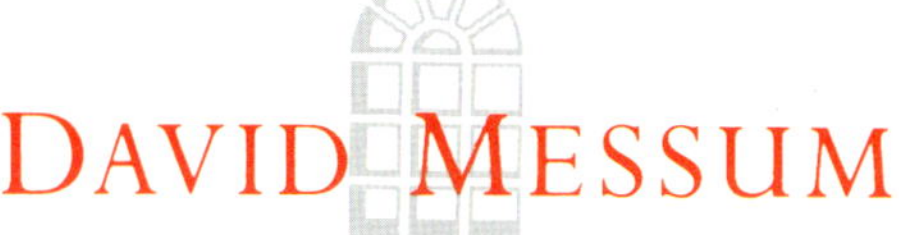

DAVID MESSUM
Fine Art
40 Duke Street, St. James's, London SW1Y 6DF
Telephone: +44 (0)171-839 5180

Foreword

JUST occasionally within our midst there comes a genius, but they are not always so easy to recognise. With no interest in fame and their talents openly given, they provide succour to those around but little immediate comfort for themselves. Nothing changes – it is the same now as in Churchyard's time, two hundred years ago. As ever, it is easier now with the benefit of hindsight to recognise that generosity of spirit which can be found in both the life and work of Thomas Churchyard. He was a devoted father to a large family, a successful lawyer, a *"Woodbridge Wit"*, a dedicated artist and collector.

Perhaps his fault was to like life too much, but whatever, he has left us an amazing legacy in his lifetime's work which in itself speaks of the joys he found in landscape painting predominately around his home town of Woodbridge, Suffolk.

It is only now in his bicentenary year that the world has begun to value him – but it has not been that easy to unravel this genius as his work has often been clouded in confusion.

The greatest body of his oeuvre came into being in the last twenty or so years of his life, consisting mostly of sketch book size watercolours and drawings. It was these that formed the legacy (for he sold very little in his lifetime) to his seven daughters, bound into Albums and dedicated to each child. None of the daughters married and the Albums remained virtually intact within the family until 1927. Following the death of Harriet, the last surviving daughter, the Churchyard family estate and practically his whole life's work along with his children's was put under the hammer. On Monday April 11th 1927 Messrs, Arnott and Everett successfully "knocked down" to the assembled company the work of a life-time, which was then inevitably dispersed far and wide. So good was his work, that once taken from the Albums, he was often confused with greater names such as Constable, Cotman and Crome. With the identity of his work suspended in confusion, it has taken time for greater knowledge of his output to become known and his paintings correctly re-ascribed to him.

The two Albums from which this catalogue is drawn are a recent discovery. Purchased at that 1927 sale by Agnes Shaw (née Airy) they have remained in the same family until this day and provide the clearest view of the artist's work from an unimpeachable source. In their entirety they demonstrate the genius of an English artist of demure aspirations, a contemporary of some of our greatest landscape painters, who wished only to paint whatever he saw, and whose talents are only just beginning to be appreciated.

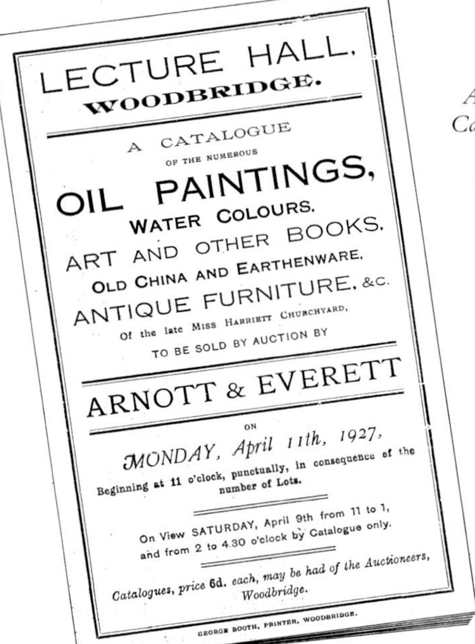
LECTURE HALL,
WOODBRIDGE.
A CATALOGUE
OF THE NUMEROUS
OIL PAINTINGS,
WATER COLOURS.
ART AND OTHER BOOKS.
OLD CHINA AND EARTHENWARE.
ANTIQUE FURNITURE, &c.
Of the late MISS HARRIETT CHURCHYARD,
TO BE SOLD BY AUCTION BY
ARNOTT & EVERETT
ON
MONDAY, April 11th, 1927,
Beginning at 11 o'clock, punctually, in consequence of the number of Lots.
On View SATURDAY, April 9th from 11 to 1, and from 2 to 4.30 o'clock by Catalogue only.
Catalogues, price 6d. each, may be had of the Auctioneers, Woodbridge.
GEORGE BOOTH, PRINTER, WOODBRIDGE.

Arnott & Everett Sale Catalogue, April 1927, in which the Albums were included for sale

We are indebted to Stephen Reiss, whose friendship and endless energy have made this exhibition possible. He for his part wishes to place on record the crucial help of Norman Scharfe whose knowledge of Suffolk topography and history is unique. Nearly all the works have been identified and catalogued accordingly, allowing the layout to clearly identify the artist's painting grounds. It has been no ordinary job, but an adventure of dedication, commitment and generosity of spirit for which we thank them greatly. *DM*

Bibliography

Among the many books and pamphlets we have consulted in the preparation of this catalogue we would particularly mention: Denis Thomas *Thomas Churchyard of Woodbridge* Chislehurst 1966; Wallace Morfey *Painting the Day, Thomas Churchyard* Woodbridge 1986; Robert Blake *The Search for Thomas Churchyard* Brightlingsea 1997; Hugh Belsey *Thomas Churchyard* Bicentenary Exhibition Catalogue, Ipswich 1998.

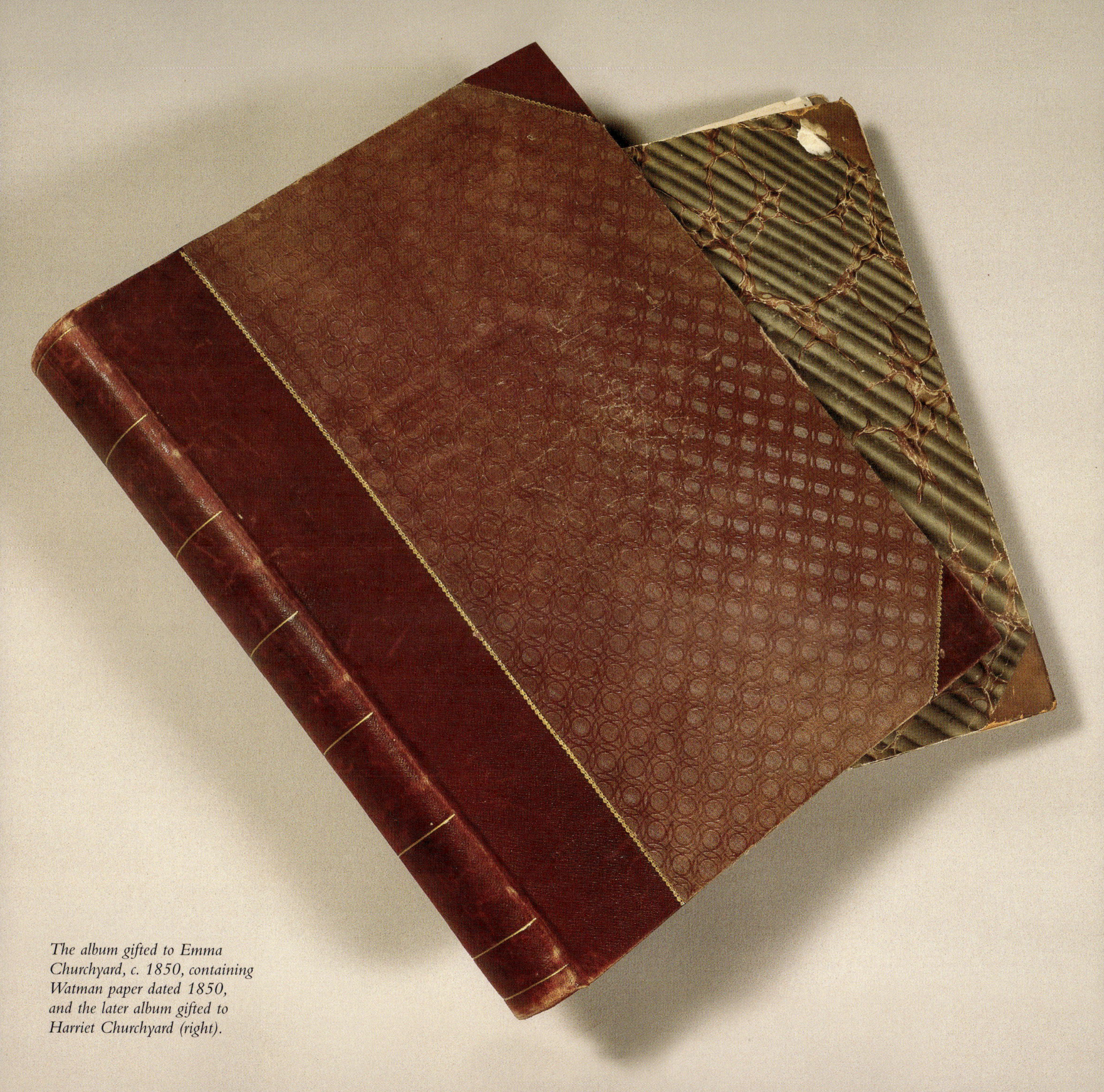

The album gifted to Emma Churchyard, c. 1850, containing Watman paper dated 1850, and the later album gifted to Harriet Churchyard (right).

Woodbridge and the Deben

Provenance of the watercolours in this section:

Nos. 1-28 The Emma Churchyard Album, then to Elizabeth (Bessie) Churchyard and then to Harriet Churchyard, then to Agnes Shaw (née Airy) and thence by descent.

Nos. 29-30 As catalogued.

Nos. 31-46 The Harriet Churchyard Album, then to Agnes Shaw (née Airy) and thence by descent.

1. JESSUP'S QUAY, WOODBRIDGE
Watercolour 3¾ x 4¾ ins *(Ref. D3)*
Inscribed *Woodbridge Quay*

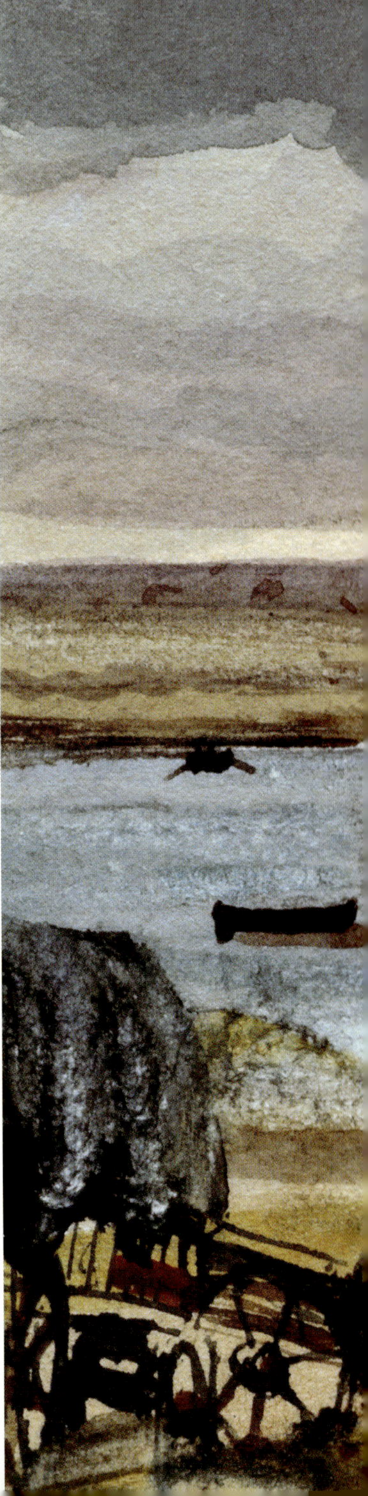

THOMAS CHURCHYARD, whose bicentenary we celebrate, was one of the most engaging characters in the history of art. His love of painting was so great that he cheerfully let it wreck a promising legal career and repeatedly drive him into debt. Yet he was never to forfeit the affection of his numerous family or of the community in which he lived. His eloquence and generosity as an advocate, his championship of the underprivileged, and his transparent honesty endeared him to all who knew him. They saw him as an outstanding connoisseur of paintings, a great collector, an inveterate sketcher, and a talented solicitor whose rare presence at the office was an accepted part of Woodbridge life.

Born in 1798 in Melton, a village just north of the Suffolk market town of Woodbridge, he was the only child of a meat trader whose business had prospered during the Napoleonic wars. Wishing to give Thomas the best possible start in life, he sent him as a boarder to Dedham Grammar School, where John Constable had been a pupil twenty years earlier, and in 1816 to Halesworth, another market town several miles to

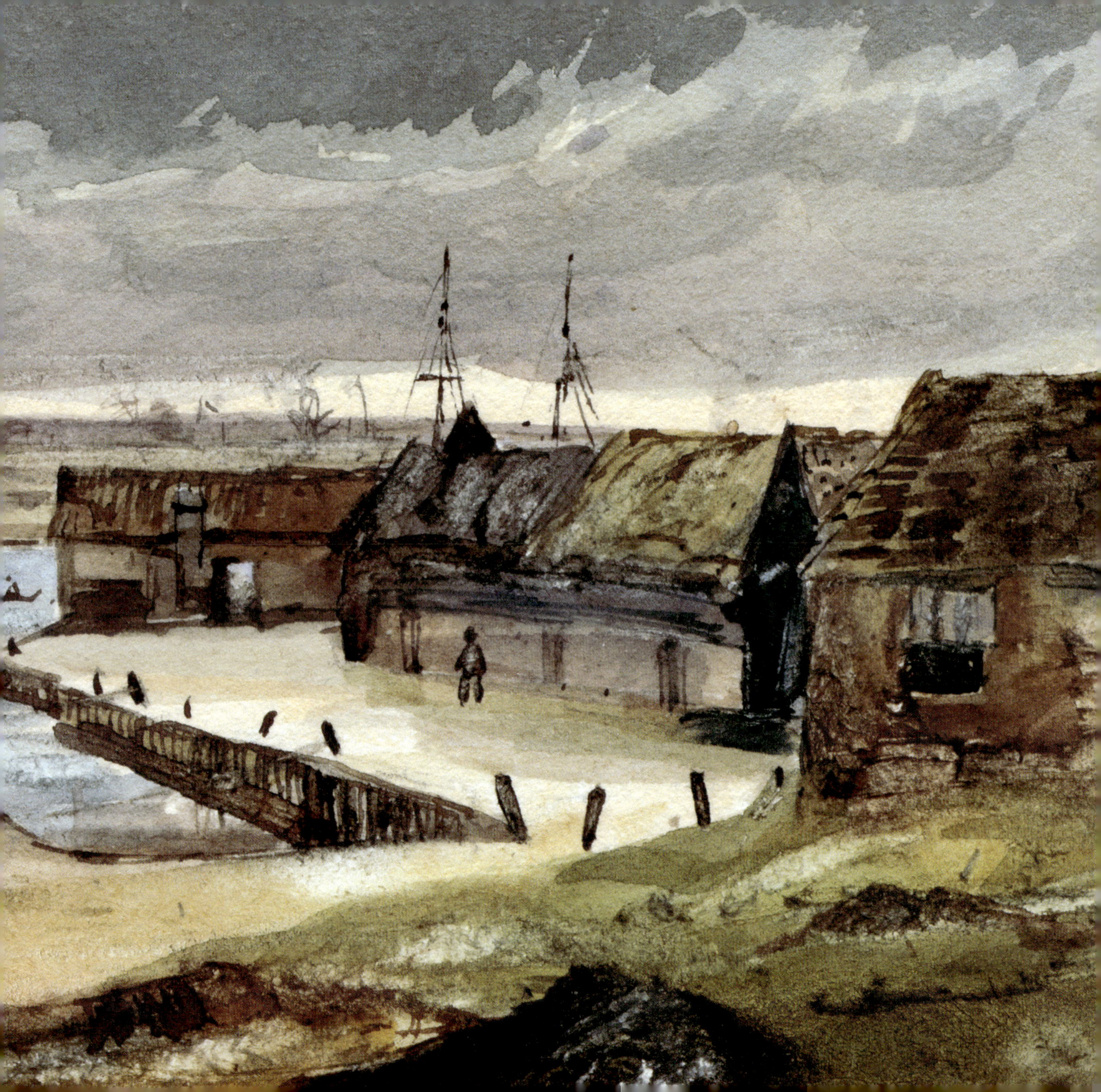

the north, to be articled to a firm of solicitors. His training ended with a year in London and, in 1822, he set up as a solicitor in Woodbridge. He secretly married in London in 1825 and two months later his first child was born. At some stage however, it is not quite certain when, he contracted an overwhelming desire to devote his life to painting, both as performer and collector. In 1829 four of his paintings were hung in the annual exhibition of the Norwich Society of Artists and were so well received that he was promptly invited to become an honorary member of the Society, a signal honour for a newcomer. Then, the following year, three of his pictures were accepted and exhibited at the Society of British Artists in London.

The die was cast. In 1832, at the age of 34, Churchyard gave up his prospering solicitor's practice, sold his house, his library, the pictures he had already bought and, having made sure his wife and growing family were comfortably settled in his widowed mother's house in Melton, set off for London to become a full-time painter. Just why he returned to Woodbridge only eighteen months later is not exactly known, but it is said he was so shocked that one of Constable's finest pictures, *Helmingham Dell*, was knocked down at Christie's for only fifty shillings that he concluded the streets of London might not after all be paved with gold. As it happens, the price had been the result of a bizarre set of circumstances and was unrepresentative. Nevertheless return he did and at once he set about re-establishing his business as an attorney.

After an abortive partnership with two younger solicitors, he came to recognise that his eccentricities made it advisable for him to practise solo, and during the last twenty-four years of his life this decision prevailed. He in fact

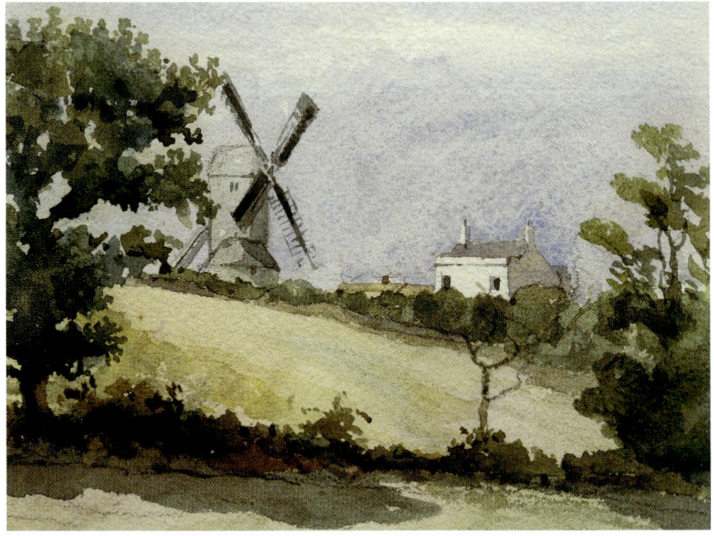

2. Postmill, Woodbridge
Watercolour 5¾ x 7¾ ins
Inscribed *at Woodbridge*
One of four windmills formerly on the high ground on the NW outskirts of town. *(Ref. C3)*

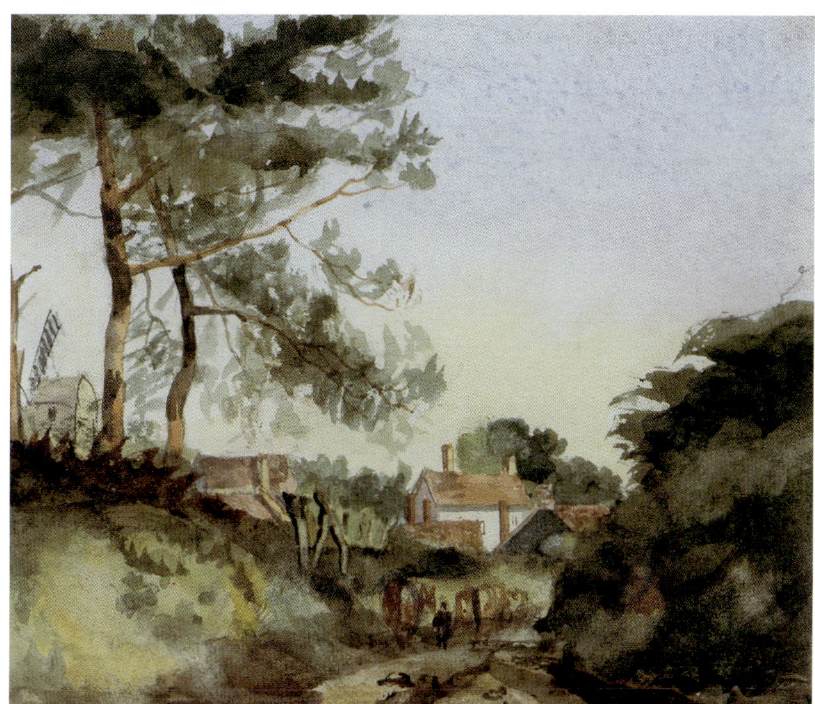

3. HAUGH LANE, WOODBRIDGE
Watercolour 5¼ x 6 ins
Inscribed *in the Haugh Lane*
The northernmost of the four windmills can be seen top left.
(Ref. C3)

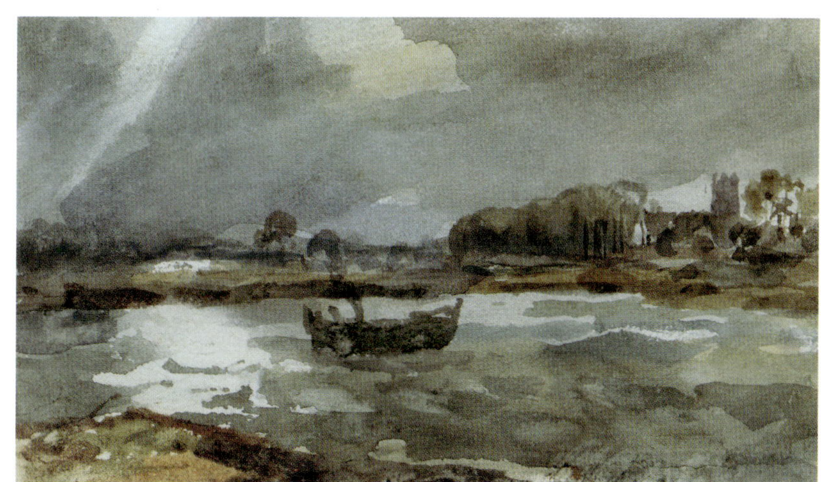

4. NIGHTFALL, THE DEBEN
Watercolour 3¾ x 6¼ ins
Inscribed *at Woodbridge*
Little of the town is visible apart from St Mary's Church. *(Ref. D3)*

concentrated almost exclusively on his skill as an advocate and avoided the hum-drum office aspects of the profession. He probably never wrote more than a couple of letters a month during his entire life; certainly none has survived. This left him comparatively free to pursue his sketching and his picture-buying whenever the spirit moved him.

His two great luminaries were Constable and Crome, and it was their work especially he bought whenever he could. However he was very far from being a mere imitator. Whereas they had seen the sketch as no more than a step towards the finished picture, the sketch for him was potentially an end in itself. In this, like Bonington, Corot and Boudin, he was a precursor of the Impressionists. To his contemporaries however, and for many at a later date, the supposed unfinished character of his work stamped him as an amateur. Thus his friend, the poet Bernard Barton, said with more than a hint of disapproval: 'Churchyard will dash you off slight and careless sketches by the dozen, or score, but for touching, retouching, or finishing this is quite another affair'. But as Churchyard was one of the first to recognise, the fresh spontaneity of the immediate impression, so crucial in the direct painting of nature, is literally fugitive and can all too often disappear in the process of completion. Sometimes it is thought that the sketch is of its nature lightweight. This too is a misconception. As often as not the superficial mind seeks to

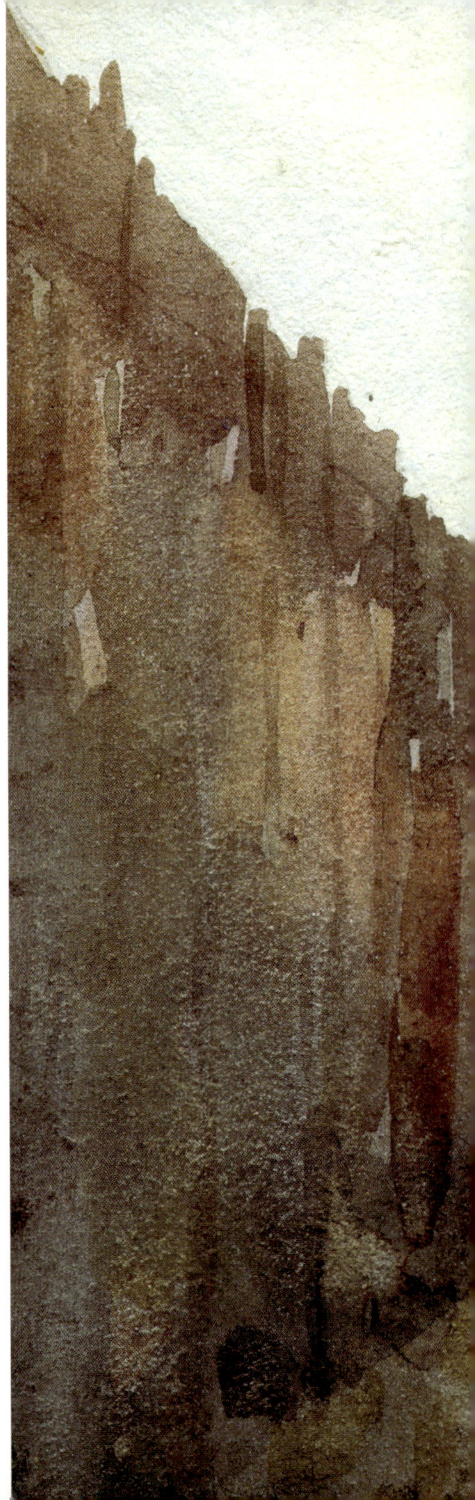

5. HORSE GRAZING, HIGH BARRIER
Watercolour 5¾ x 7¾ ins
Supposedly by the Deben but the exact location has not been identified.

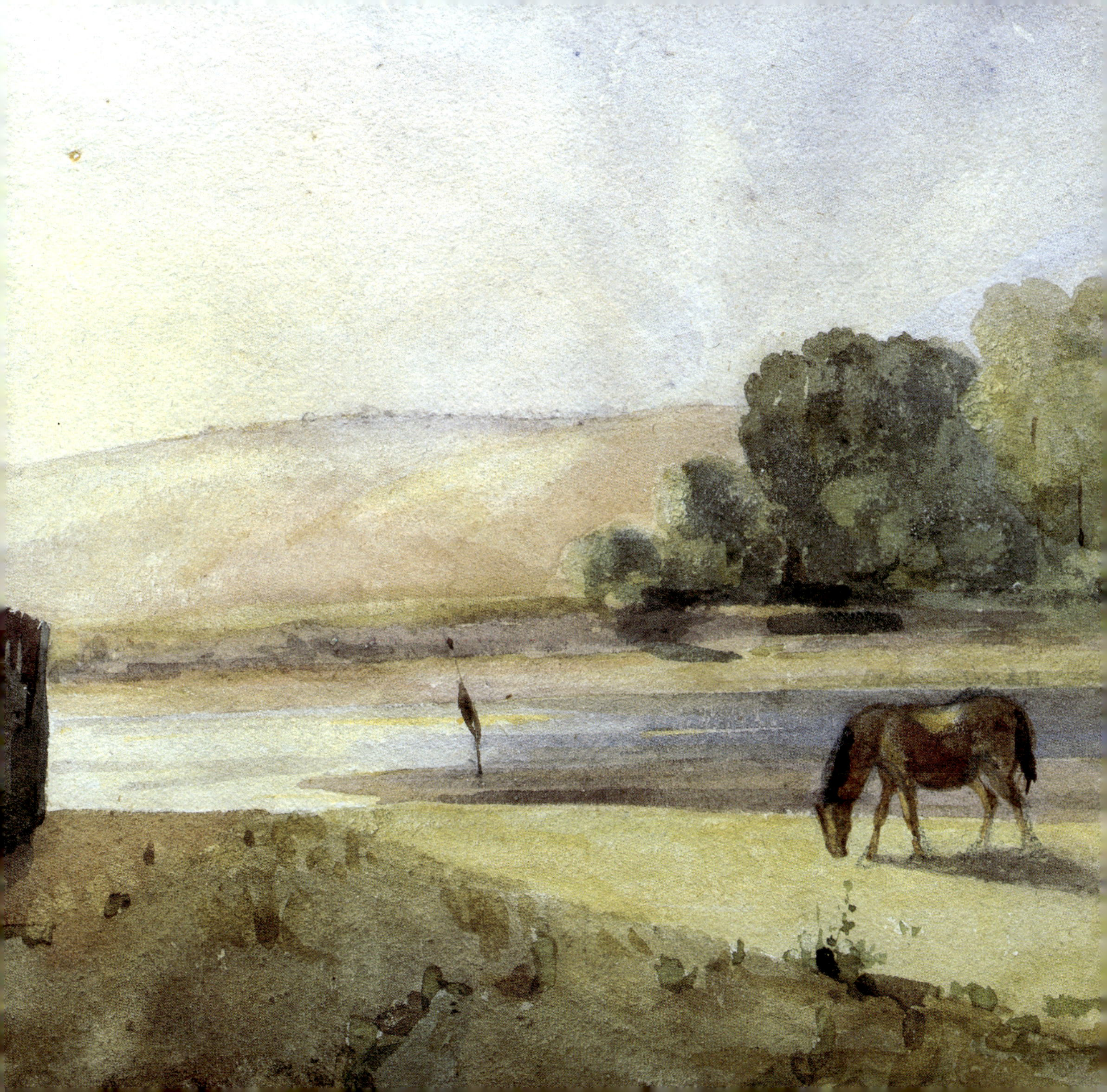

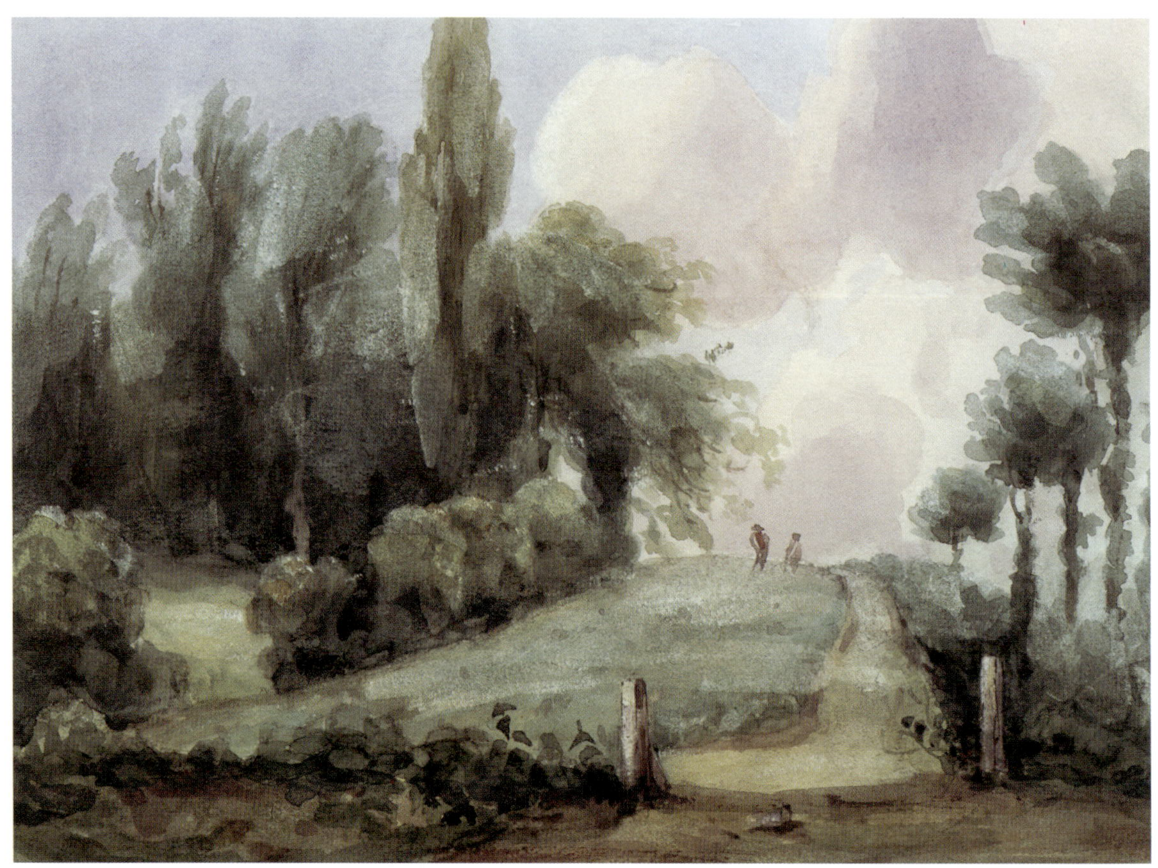

6. Approaching Kyson Point, Woodbridge
Watercolour 5¾ x 8 ins
Inscribed *at Woodbridge*
A substantial area to the south of the town is known as Kingston, with Kyson (i.e. Kingston) Point its southernmost tip. Much of the land is now owned by the National Trust. *(Ref. D3)*

impress by rhetoric whereas the deep thinker will endlessly search for the simple uncomplicated statement.

The immediacy of Churchyard's intelligence also informed his work as an advocate. This is reflected in a tribute from Judge Worlledge:

"I had the pleasure of knowing the late Mr Churchyard for many years, both privately and in his public capacity. In his private capacity I have appreciated his refined mind, his genial spirit, and his courteous manner, but it was chiefly as an advocate in this court that I valued him: for while he did his duty fearlessly and ably to his clients, he never tried to mislead me or to overreach his opponents by unworthy arts; and he never wasted the public time by keeping up useless discussion. In him I have lost a most valuable aid in the discharge of my duty to the public in the administration of justice."

Never wasted the public time by keeping up useless discussion – this could well have been his epitaph. What Judge Worlledge probably did not fully appreciate was the extent to which Churchyard was himself only too anxious to get away and return to his beloved countryside!

But if Churchyard has been unlucky to be treated as an amateur, an understanding of his achievement has suffered even more by another quite separate sequence of misfortunes.

The story begins with his own curious reluctance to exhibit his work. There is nothing to suggest he was covetous in relation to his productions or that he felt slighted by their reception. On the contrary they were generally well received. The honour bestowed on him in 1829 by the Norwich Society of Artists has already been mentioned. Yet Churchyard never exhibited with the Society again. For three years only did he exhibit in London, eleven pictures in

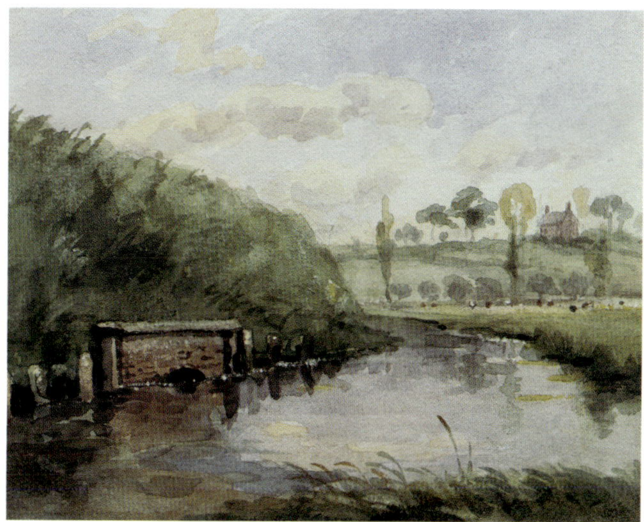

7. A Narrow Stretch of the Deben
Watercolour 3¾ x 4¾ ins
Inscribed *at Woodbridge*

8. The Deben at Kingston, Woodbridge
Watercolour 3¾ x 4¾ ins
Inscribed *at Kingston, Woodbridge*
Kyson Point lower right. *(Ref. D3)*

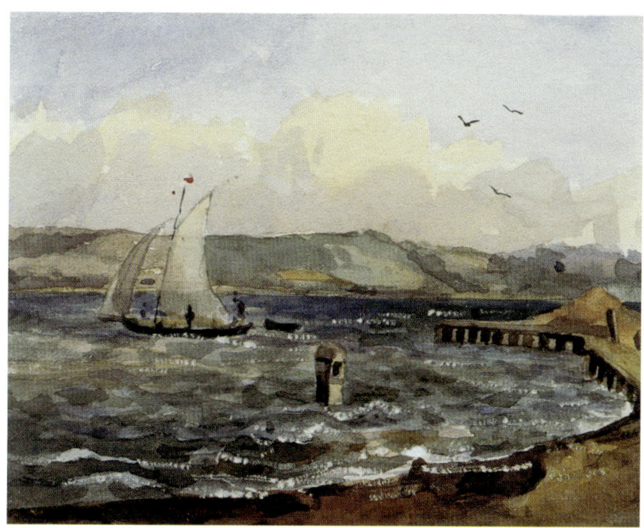

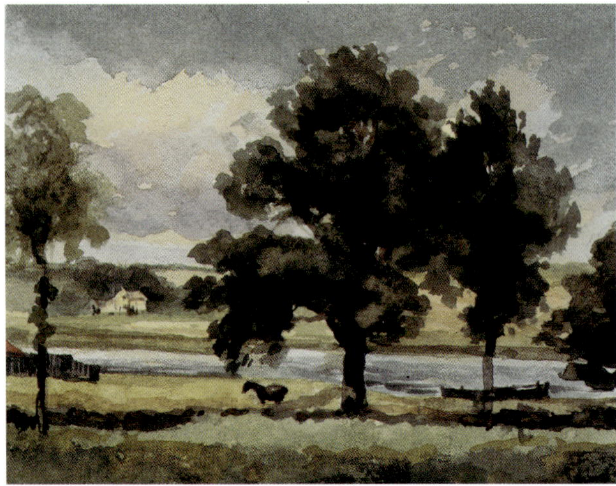

9. View from Mr Thomas's Garden
Watercolour 3½ x 4¾ ins
Inscribed *from Mr Thomas's Garden, Woodbridge*
George Thomas had a house on the Thoroughfare (the main street) towards the N.E. of the town. His name is listed in the 1844 Directory but not in that of 1855. From 1859 onwards the view was interrupted by the railway which ran parallel with the river approximately where the horse is standing. A date *circa* 1850 can therefore be assumed. *(Ref. C3)*

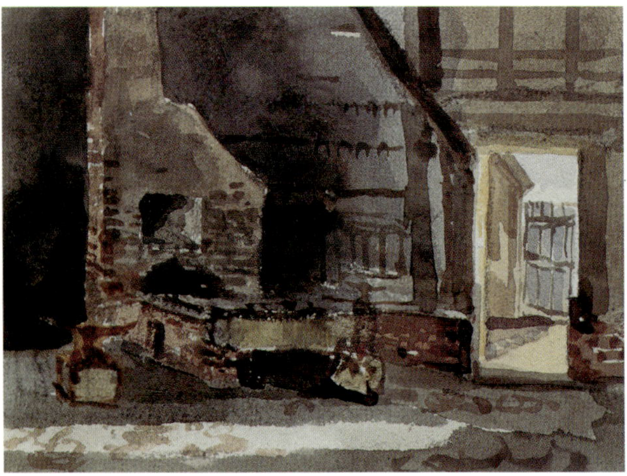

10. Blacksmith's Shop, Woodbridge
Watercolour 3½ x 4¾ ins
Inscribed *Blacksmith's Shop, Woodbridge*
There were four blacksmiths in Woodbridge in 1855, the approximate date of this picture.

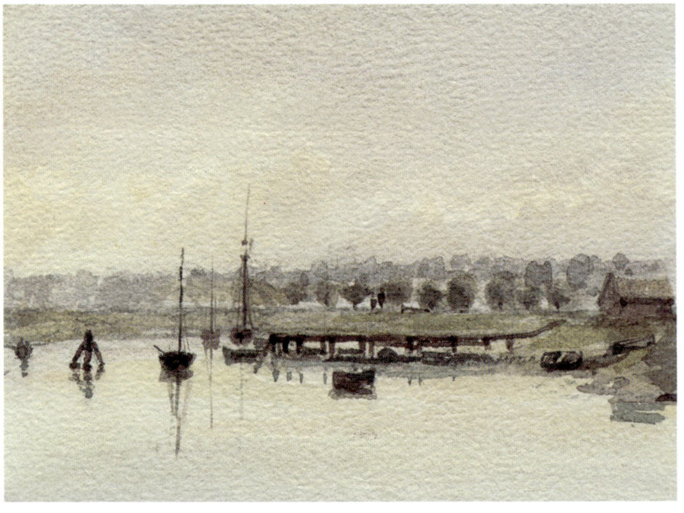

11. Everson's Jetty, Woodbridge
Watercolour 3¾ x 4¾ ins
Inscribed *Woodbridge Jetty*
Close to what is now the Woodbridge Yacht Club. *(Ref. D3)*

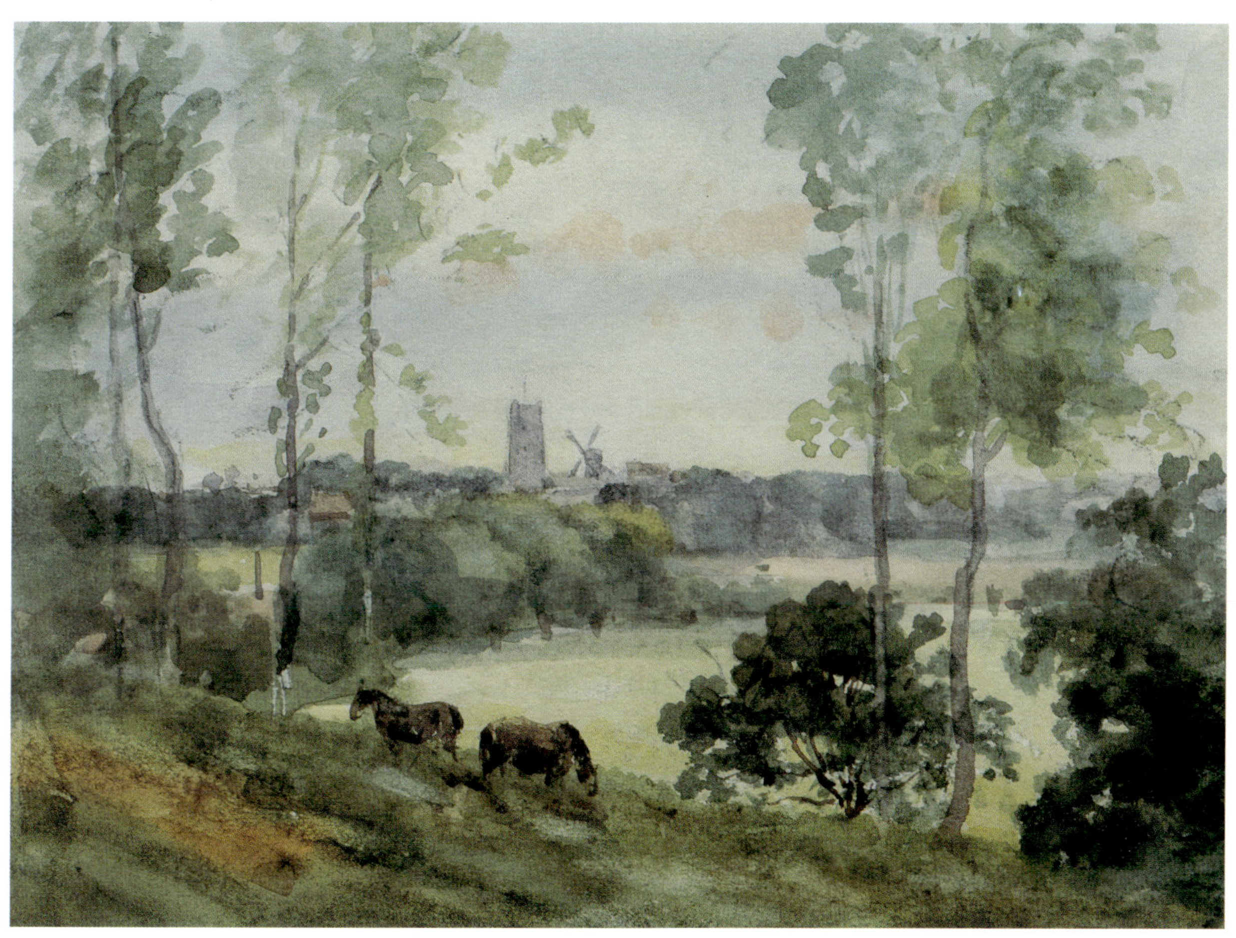

12. View from the East Bank of the Deben
Watercolour 5¾ x 7¾ ins
Tricker's Windmill and the Shire Hall can be seen to the right of St Mary's Church. *(Ref. D3)*

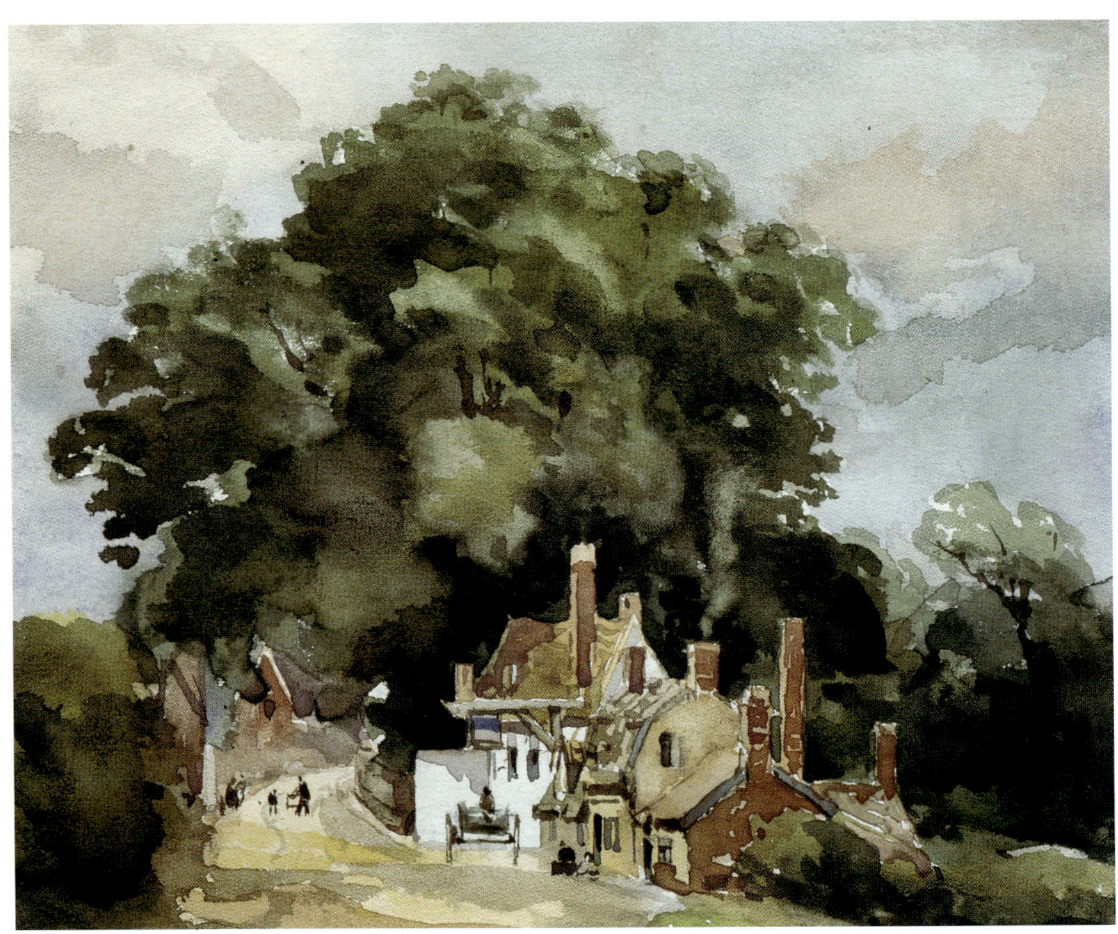

13. Cherry Tree Inn I
Watercolour 5¾ x 6¾ ins
At the time, *circa* 1850, Churchyard was living out of sight in Cumberland Street. An oil version of this subject is seen on the back cover of *The Search for Thomas Churchyard* by Robert Blake, 1998. *(Ref. D2)*

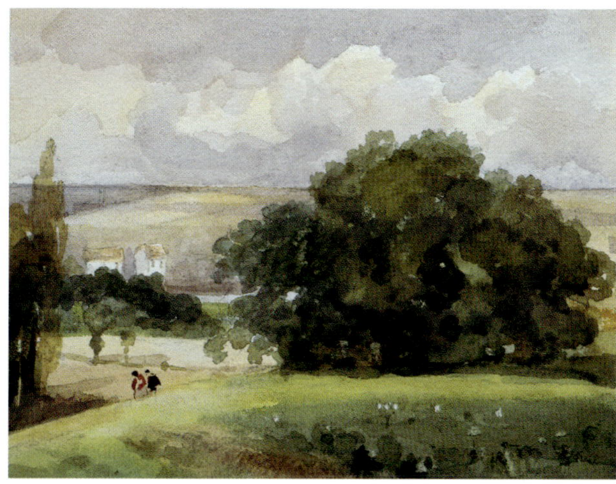

15. THE DEBEN FROM SUTTON WALKS
Watercolour 3¾ x 4¾ ins
The two buildings may be based on the Tide Mill and its warehouse. *(Ref. C4)*

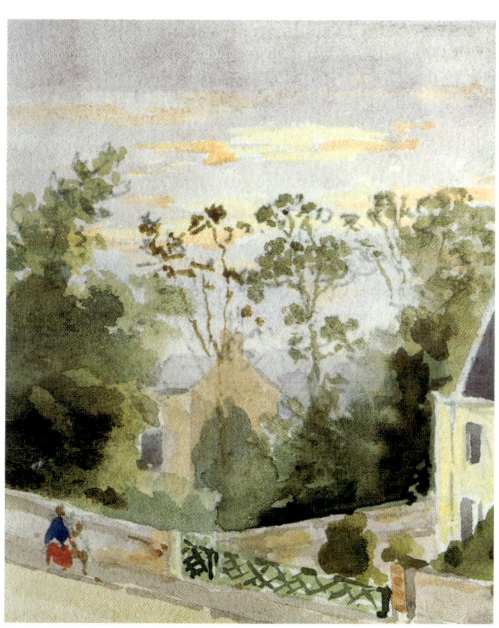

14. HOUSES ON NORTH HILL, WOODBRIDGE
Watercolour 4¾ x 3¾ ins
It is just possible the regency house may be the same as that seen in 2. *(Ref. C3)*

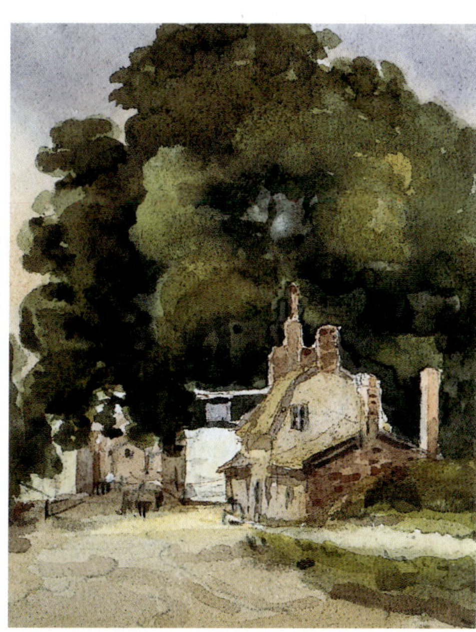

16. CHERRY TREE INN II
Watercolour 4¾ x 3¾ ins
Shows more of Cumberland Street than 13. *(Ref. D2)*

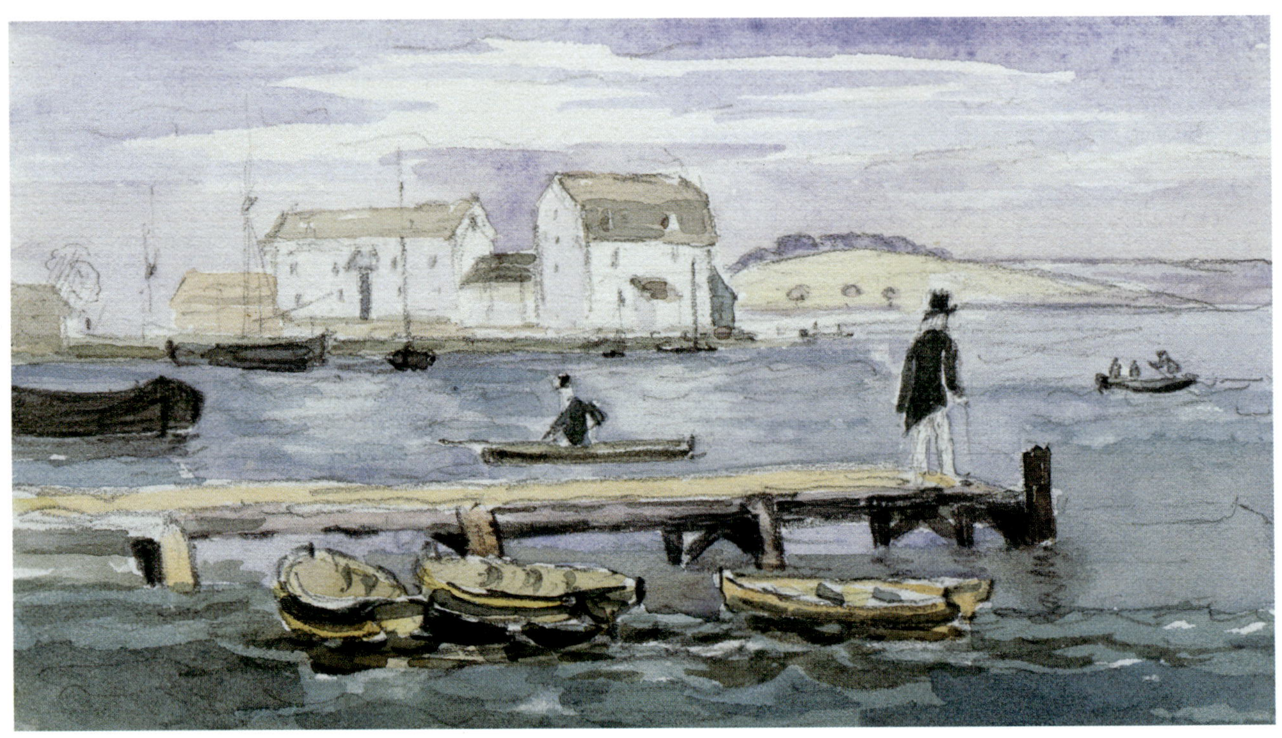

17. Woodbridge Waterfront
Watercolour 3¼ x 6 ins
Beyond the Jetty is seen one of Woodbridge's best known buildings, the 17th century Tide Mill. A Tide Mill is recorded on this site as early as 1170. *(Ref. D3)*

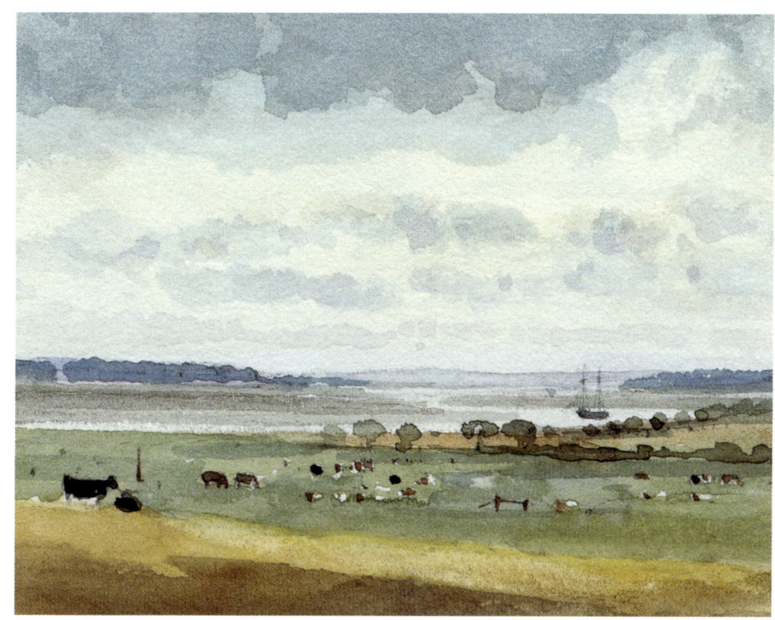

18. Deben Estuary, Cattle Foreground
Watercolour 3¾ x 4¾ ins
Probably in the vicinity of Hemley. *(Ref. F4)*

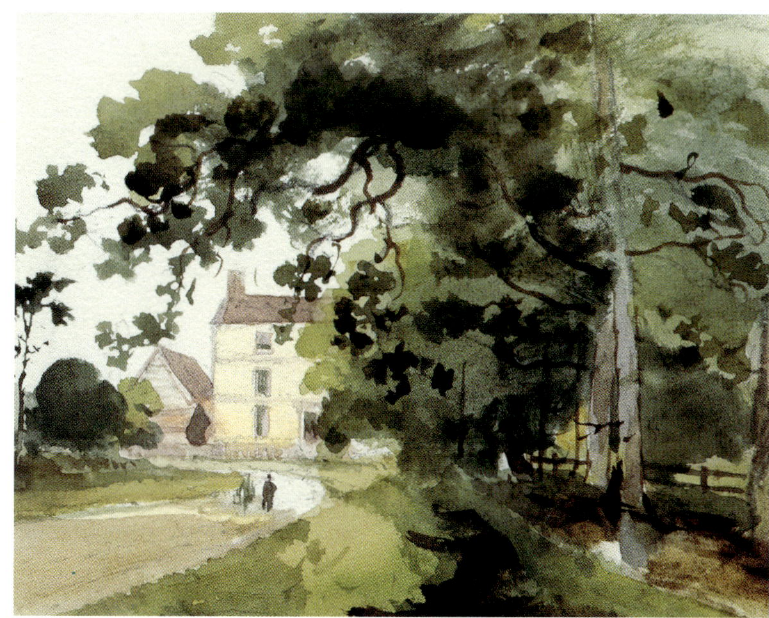

19. Kingston Farm, Woodbridge
Watercolour 3¾ x 4¾ ins
See 25. *(Ref. D3)*

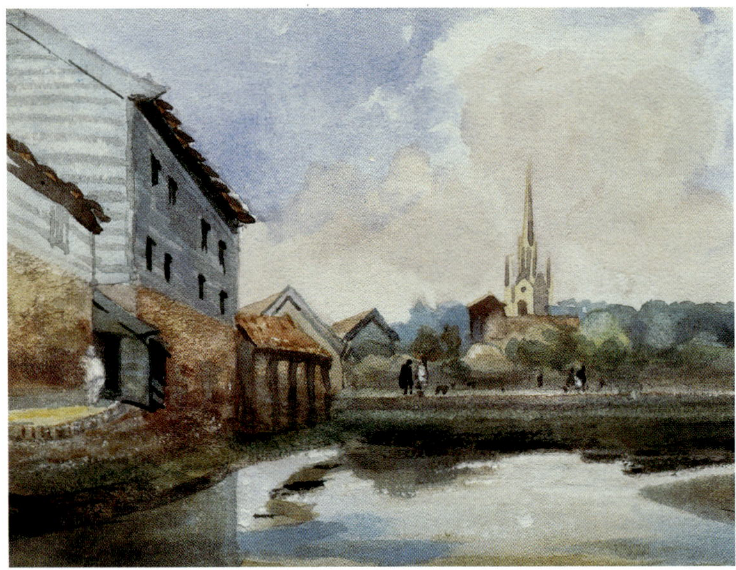

20. St. John's Church, Woodbridge
Watercolour 3¾ x 5 ins
A Victorian church built 1842-3. The spire was later removed and was not rebuilt. *(Ref. C3)*

21. Approaching Woodbridge, Ipswich Road
Watercolour 6 x 9½ ins
Note the ghost-like figures on the right, a familiar feature in Churchyard's work. The Cherry Tree Inn is just visible. *(Ref. D2)*

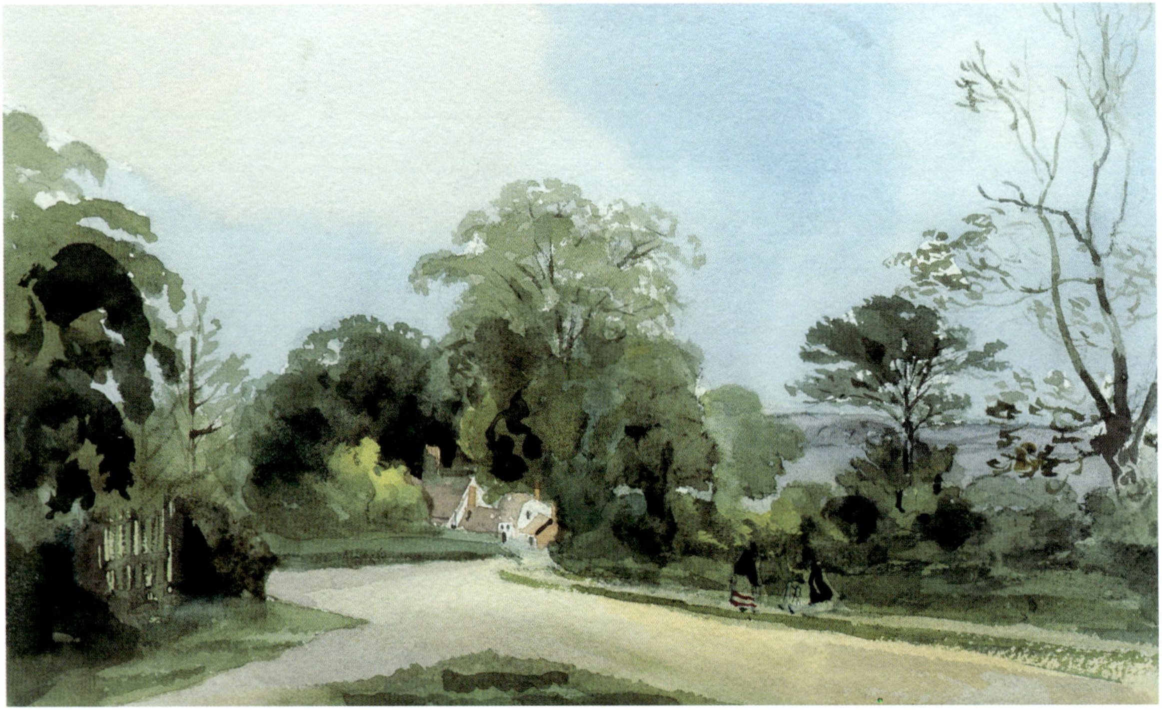

22. At the Blacksmith
Black chalk 5½ x 3½ ins

23. Two Cows by the Deben
Watercolour 5¾ x 7¾ ins
(Ref. E3)

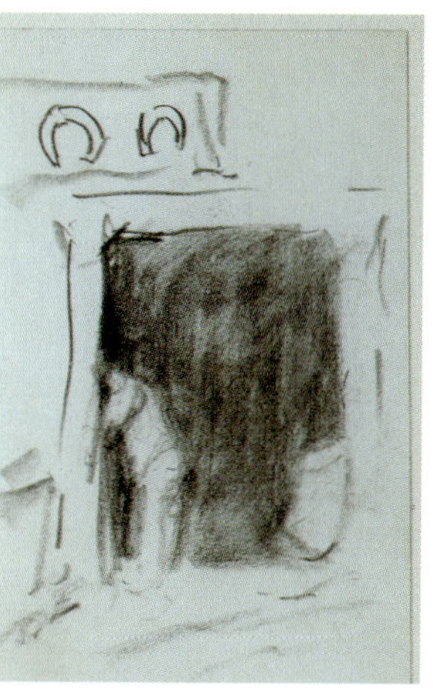

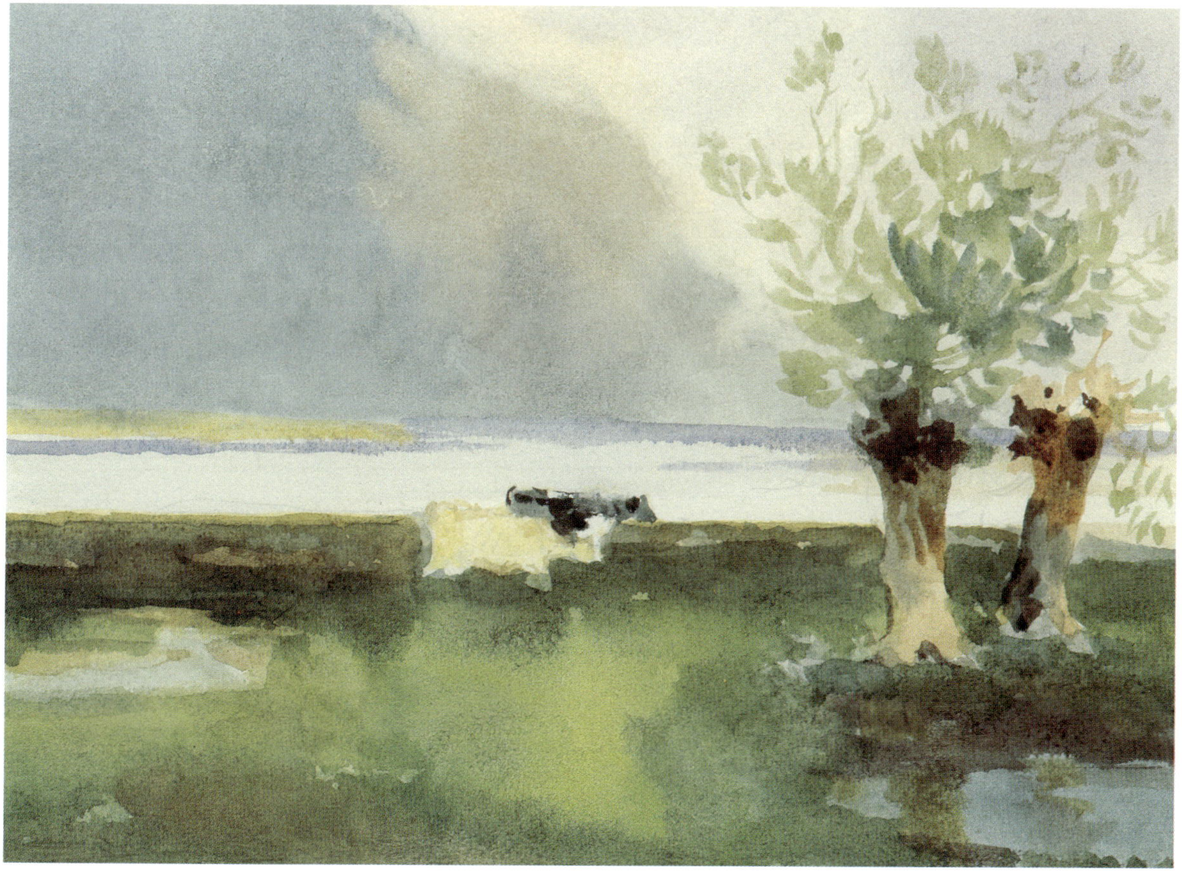

three different locations. Fifteen pictures were shown in Ipswich in 1850 under the auspices of the newly formed Suffolk Fine Arts Association, but never again. Eight were exhibited in Norwich in 1852 with the rival Norfolk and Norwich Association for the Promotion of Fine Arts, but again silence. Finally a small group appeared at the oddly named Industrial Exhibition in Woodbridge in 1865, the year he died aged sixty-seven. He was truly an eccentric.

A knowledge of these forty or so pictures would in theory provide an invaluable starting point for the study of Churchyard's stylistic evolution. Unfortunately, however, the early descriptions are too vague to permit recognition and only one picture can now be linked to a specific appearance, exhibition or otherwise, before the artist died in 1865. Another difficulty is the fact that the artist very rarely signed or dated his pictures. On the other hand, shortly before he died, he did write the name of each of his seven daughters on the back of several hundred of his pictures as well as give them each two guard-books containing at least a hundred of his watercolours and drawings. As a result any picture genuinely inscribed with a daughter's name, or known to have come from one of these fourteen guard-books, can safely be regarded as authentic. Unfortunately, however, most of the guard-books were dismembered before a record of their contents had been made, and the reliability of inscriptions is notoriously difficult to establish.

It has generally been assumed that Churchyard put names on the pictures to save argument when he was no longer there to arbitrate, but in fact there was a more pressing reason. Such were his debts that, had he not distributed his pictures

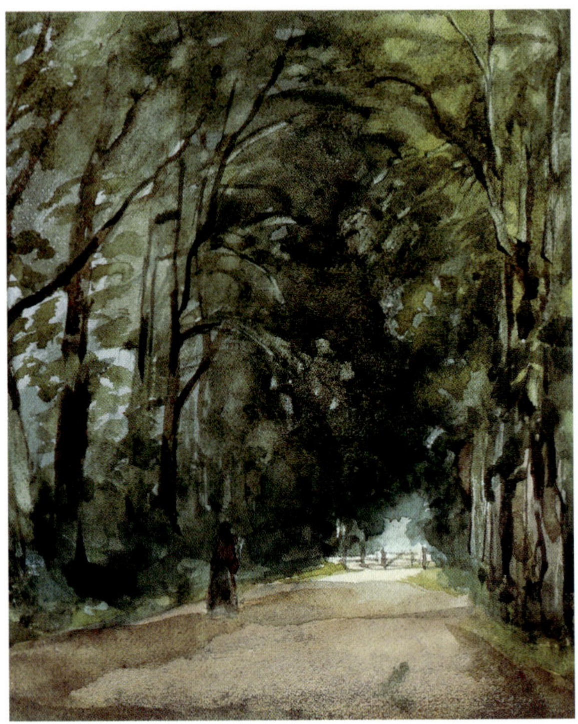

24. Jetty Lane, Woodbridge
Watercolour 4¾ x 3¾ ins
Now known as the Avenue. It leads off the Kingston Farm Road. *(Ref. D3)*

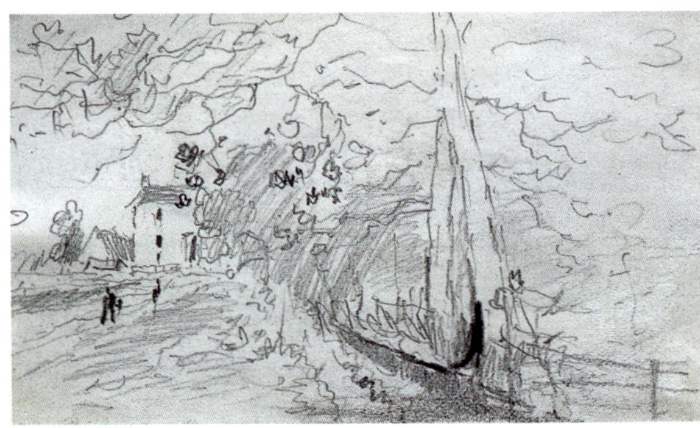

25. Approach to Kingston Farm
Pencil 2½ x 4¼ ins
A study for 19. *(Ref. D3)*

to his daughters before he died, they would necessarily have been sold for the benefit of his creditors.

None of his daughters married. In order of birth their names were Ellen, Emma, Laura, Anna, Bessie, Harriet and Kate. He also had two sons, Tom who was the eldest member of the family, and Charley the youngest. Tom had taken to farming and had migrated to Canada. Charley set out to be a solicitor but failed his exams; it seems for the rest of his life he sponged on his wealthy relatives. Neither of the sons participated in their father's picture distribution.

But what were his daughters supposed to do with their pictures? In the event they sold a few and gave a few away as presents, but the vast majority they kept. When in turn they died, their pictures were split between the others. Emma died first (1878), to be followed by Kate (1889), Laura (1891), Anna (1897), Ellen (1909), Bessie (1913) and finally Harriet (1927). Thus a very high proportion of Churchyard's artistic output came into Harriet's possession in 1913 and stayed there until she died in 1927. Intermingled with the mass of pictures by her father, however, were a great many by other artists, some TC had acquired on his picture-buying escapades but, above all, the work of his children, for the whole family dabbled in pictorial art in varying degree.

When, therefore, Harriet died in 1927, around 90% of TC's total output had remained entirely unseen and unknown. It is only since then, in the face of enormous difficulties, that the pieces of the jigsaw are gradually being put together.

Charley was still alive when Harriet died but, with unnatural haste, he arranged an auction of

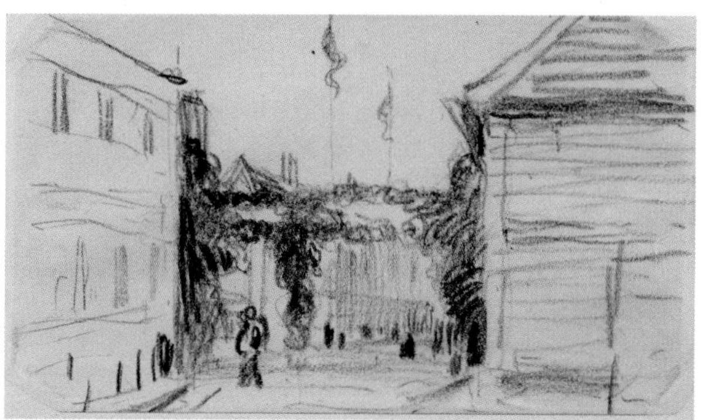

26. Celebrations, Market Hill, Woodbridge
Pencil 3¼ x 5½ ins
Shire Hall centre. The occasion is not known. *(Ref. C3)*
Verso: Cows Grazing

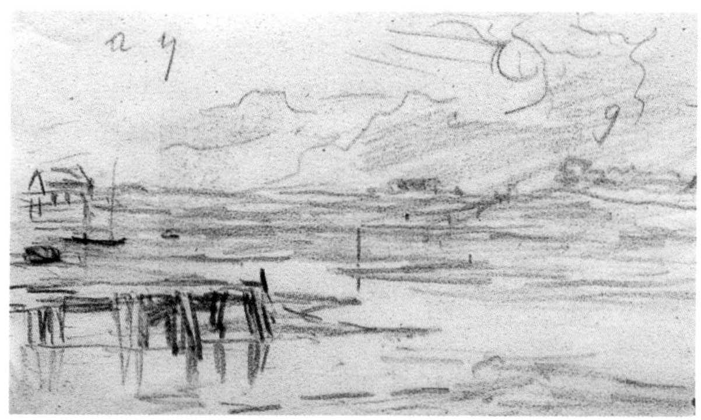

27. Everson's Jetty and Tide Mill
Pencil 3¼ x 5½ ins
A study for 17. *(Ref. D3)*

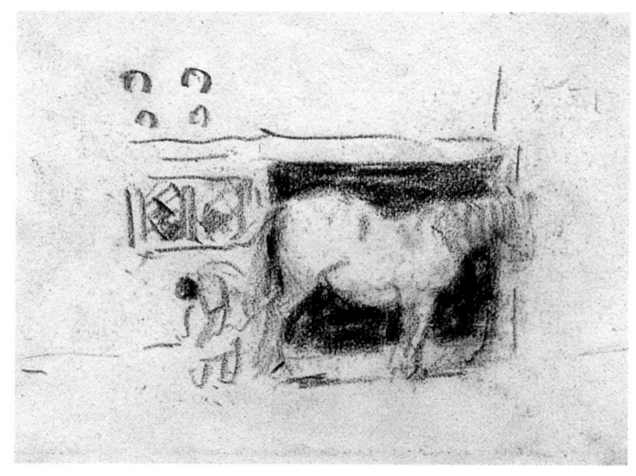

28. Shoeing the Horse
Black Chalk 3¼ x 4 ins

the entire property – mainly pictures – and this was held in Woodbridge less than three months later, on 11 April 1927. There were no reserves and all 475 lots were sold. The individual pictures were lotted into anything up to a dozen at a time, and in addition there were the guard-books, other albums, portfolios and boxes, producing a total number of pictorial items in excess of four thousand. The catalogue warned of the potential pitfalls: *Nearly all the undermentioned pictures are by members of the family of Churchyard, and many are by the late THOMAS CHURCHYARD. The initials T.C. where stated indicates that the picture is believed to be by him, but no guarantee is given.*

The whole sale, which included old china, glass, earthenware and antique furniture, realised slightly over £600, a clear indication of the current state of the Churchyard market. At this date it simply did not exist. There were a great many buyers, very few of whom were serious collectors. As a result the master's oeuvre was widely dispersed among those who had very little idea as to what they had purchased, whether by Thomas or one of his children, or by an unknown number of others, including George Frost, George Rowe, and even Constable. The process of sifting the wheat from the chaff then became doubly difficult because several of Tom's authentic pictures soon in fact graduated to Constable, his T.C. initials being mistaken for

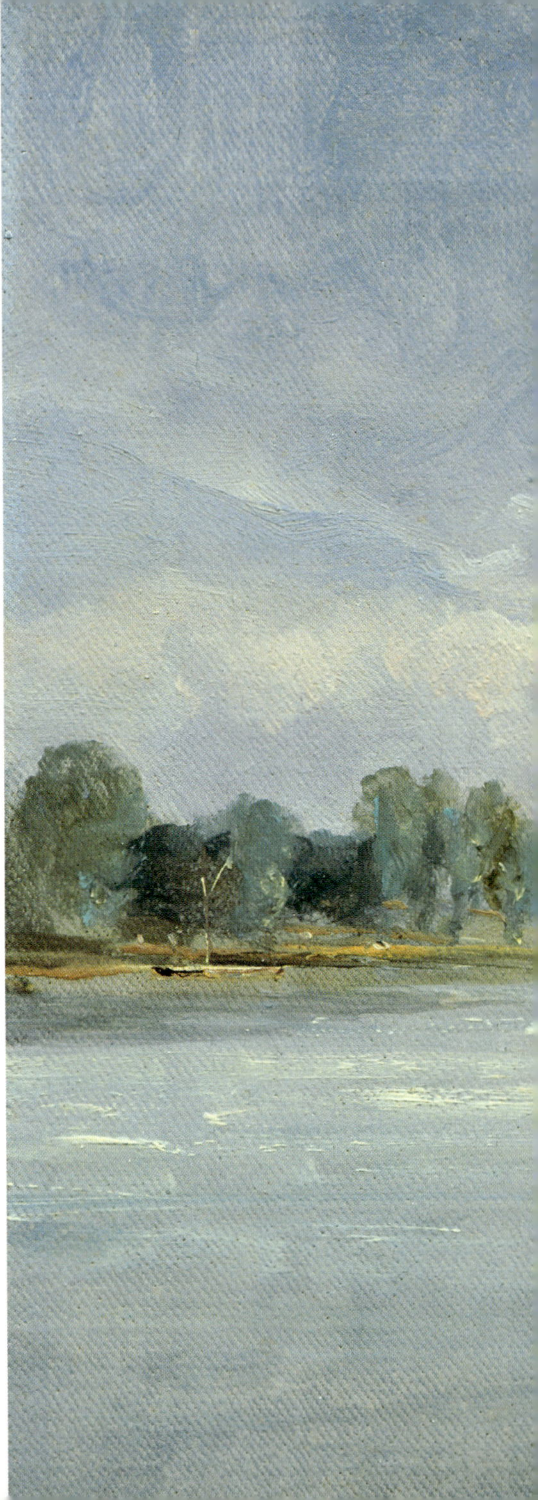

29. Limekiln Quay, Woodbridge
Oil on canvas 9 x 12¼ ins
Inscribed *Bessie Churchyard* on reverse
Looking south towards the Tide Mill the roof of which is just visible. *(Ref. C3)*
Provenance: Elizabeth Churchyard, Harriet Churchyard, Agnes Shaw, by descent.

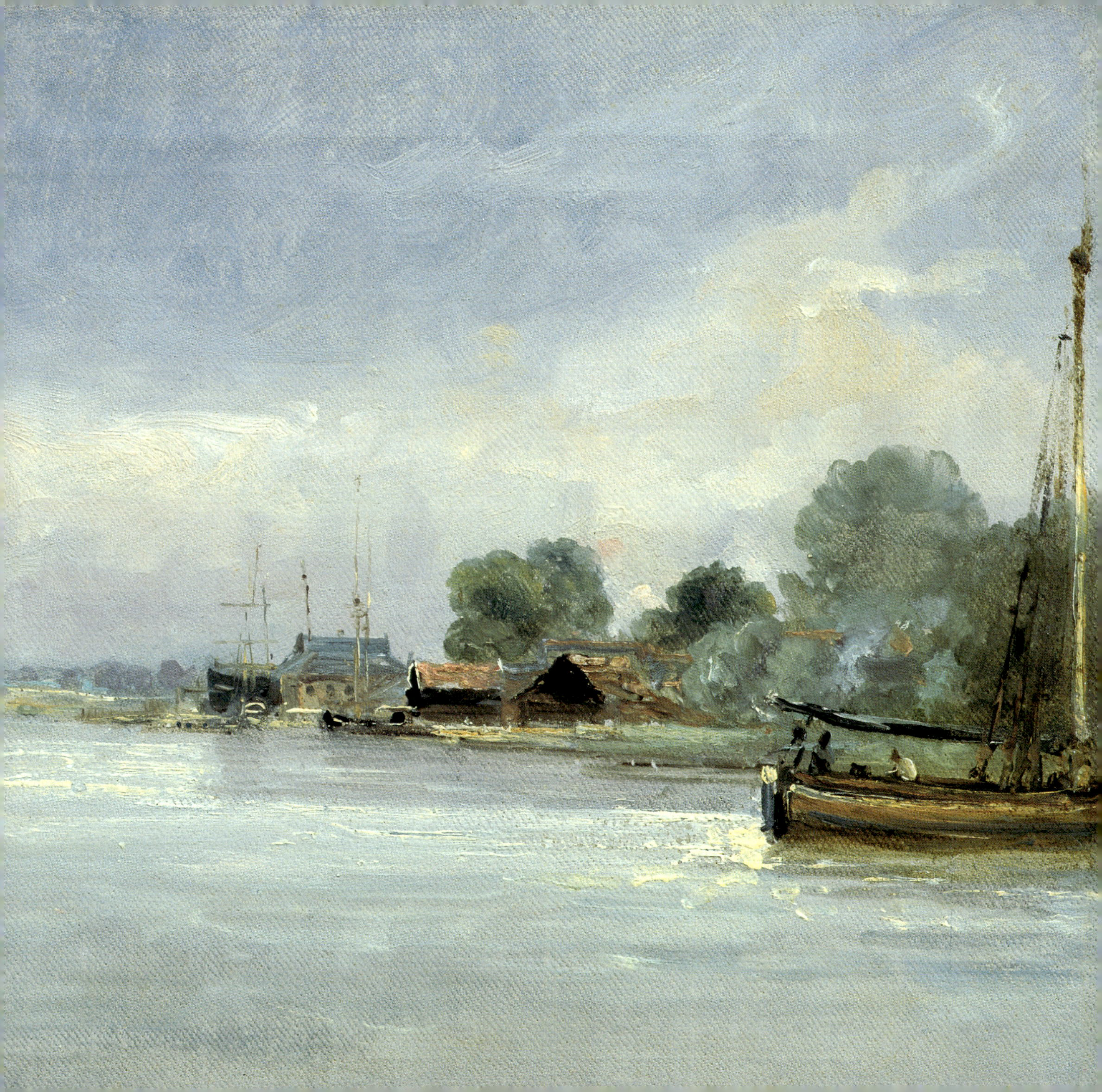

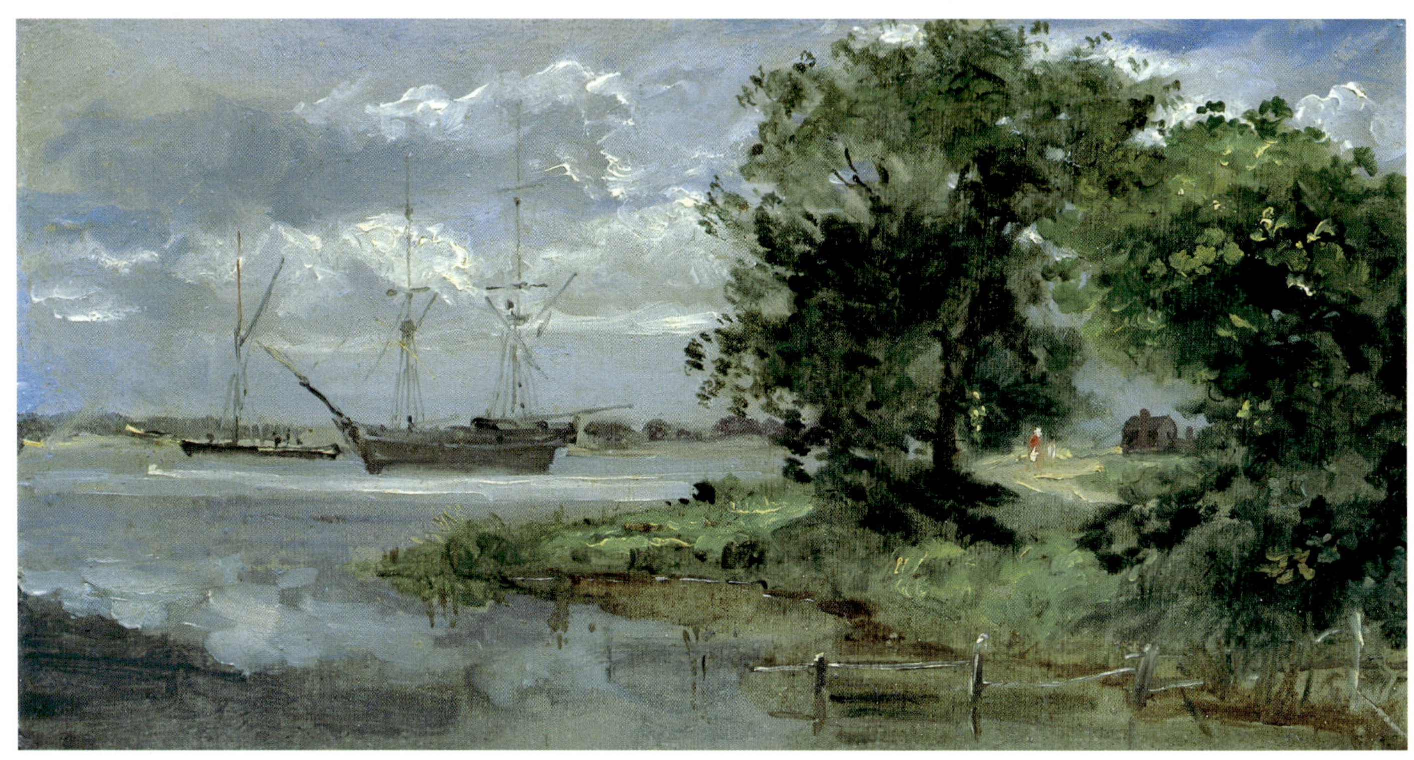

30. Kyson Point, Woodbridge
Oil on laid board 5 x 9 ins *(Ref. D3)*
Inscribed *Emma Churchyard* on reverse
Provenance: Emma Churchyard, Harriet Churchyard, Agnes Shaw, by descent.

31. Walled Garden, Woodbridge
Watercolour 3¾ x 4¾ ins

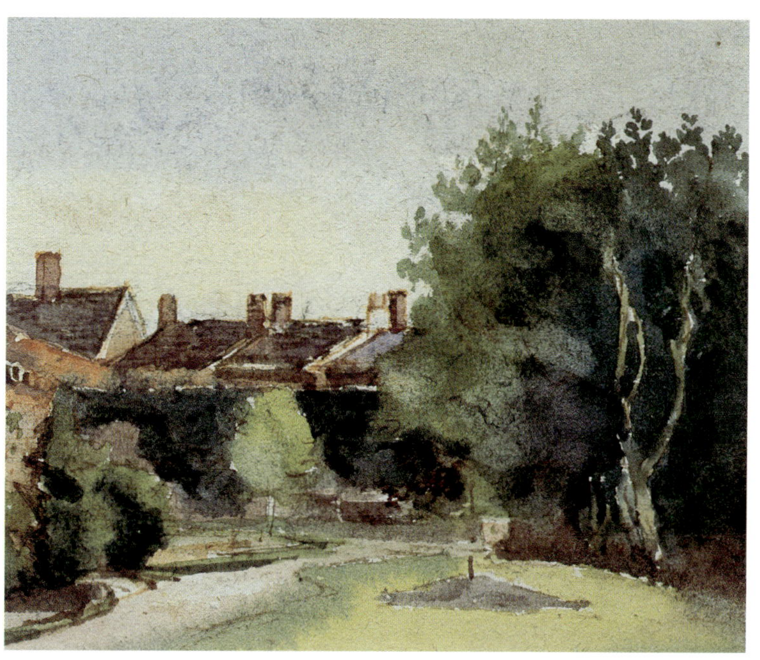

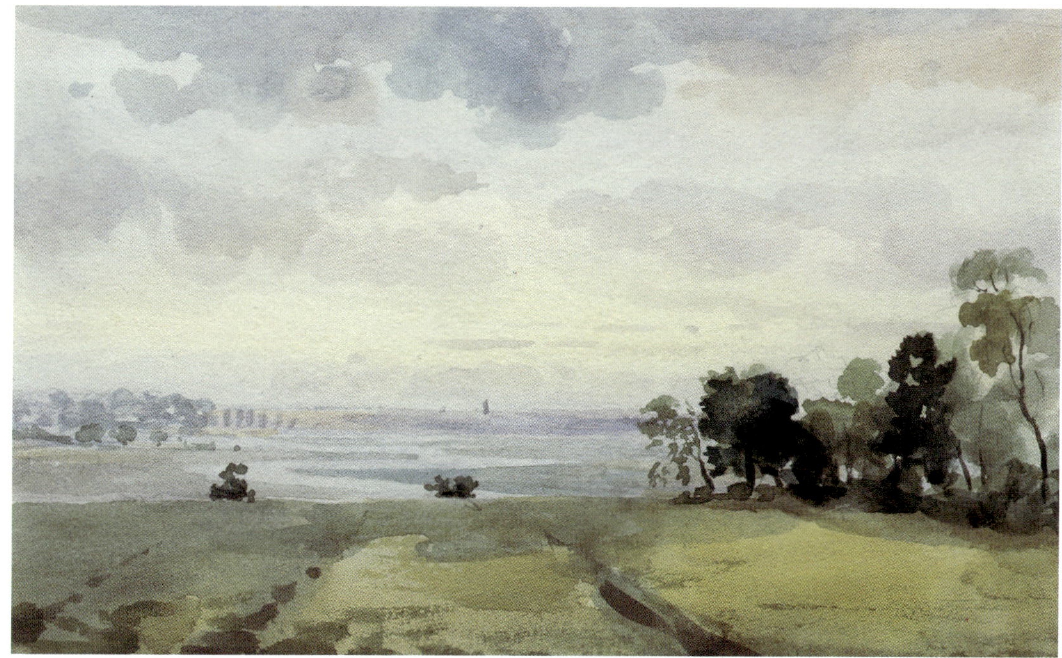

32. Dawn, Deben Estuary
Watercolour 4¾ x 7½ ins
An exceptionally low tide. *(Ref. Coast Map G2)*

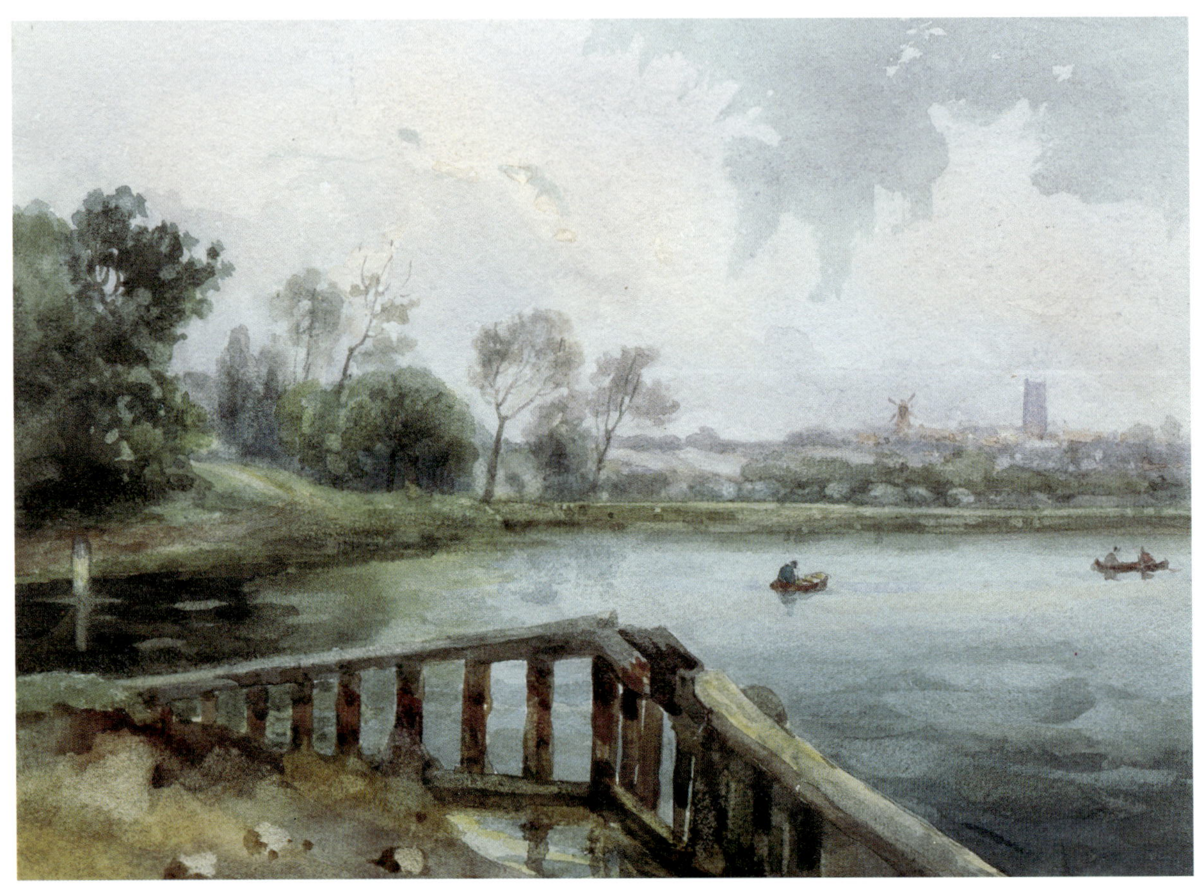

33. Woodbridge from Kyson Point
Watercolour 5¾ x 7¾ ins
See 30 and 40. *(Ref. D3)*

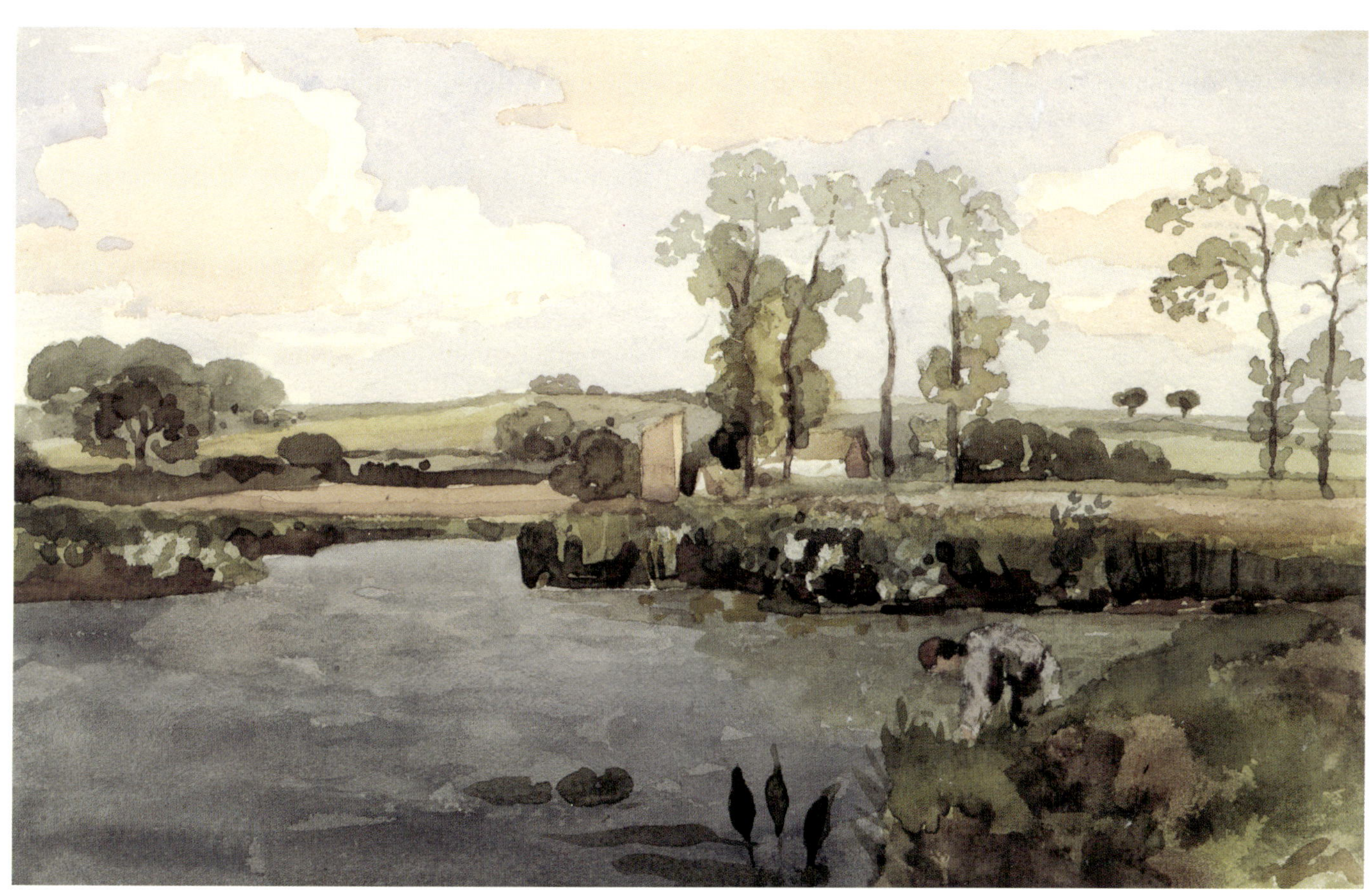

34. River Scene, Stooping Boy
Watercolour 6 x 9½ ins
Could be the Alde River and not the Deben.

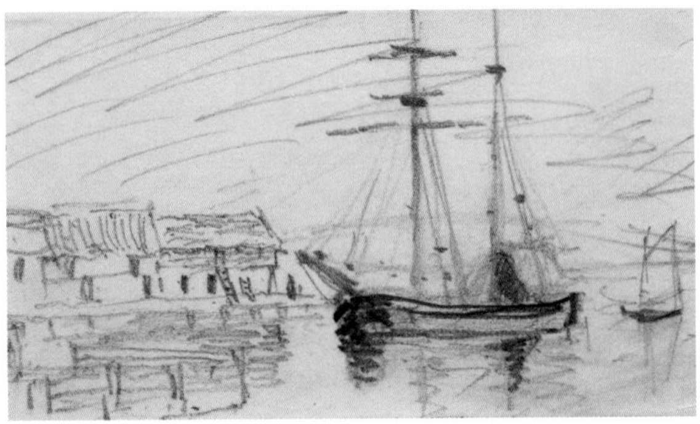

35. SCHOONER AT ANCHOR, WOODBRIDGE
Pencil 3¼ x 5¼ ins
Inscribed on reverse

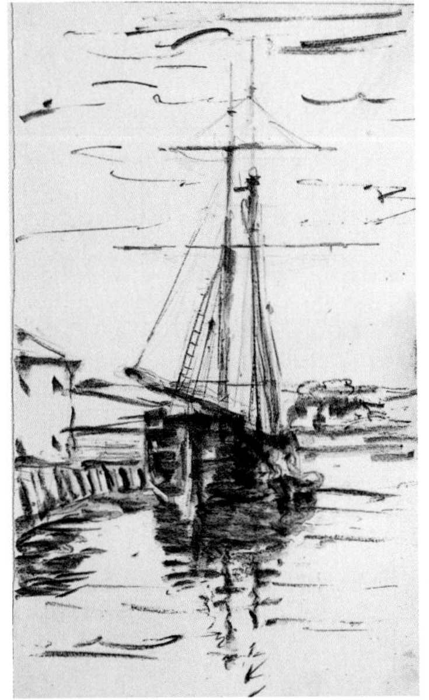

36. SAILING SHIP IN DOCK
Black chalk 7¼ x 4¼ ins
(Ref. D3)

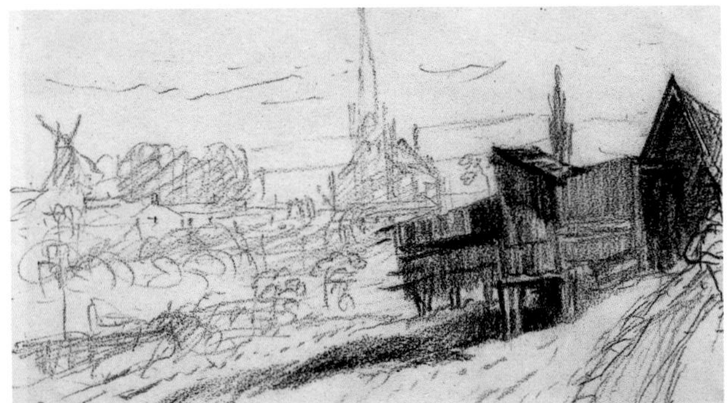

37. VIEW OF WOODBRIDGE FROM THE DOCKS
Black chalk 3¼ x 5½ ins
St John's Church spire central. *(Ref. C3)*
Verso: LANDSCAPE

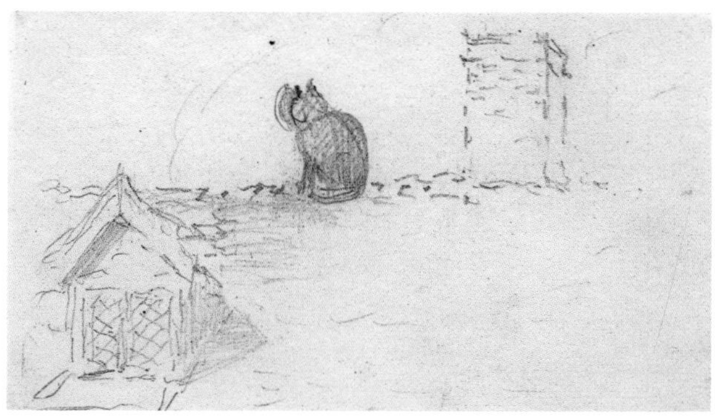

38. Cat on the Roof
Pencil 3¼ x 5½ ins
Verso: Two Figures Pencil 3 x 5 ins

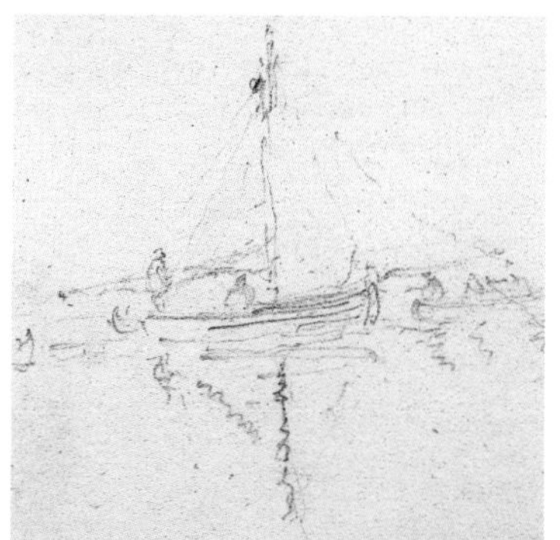

39. Repairing the Mast
Pencil 3¼ x 3¼ ins

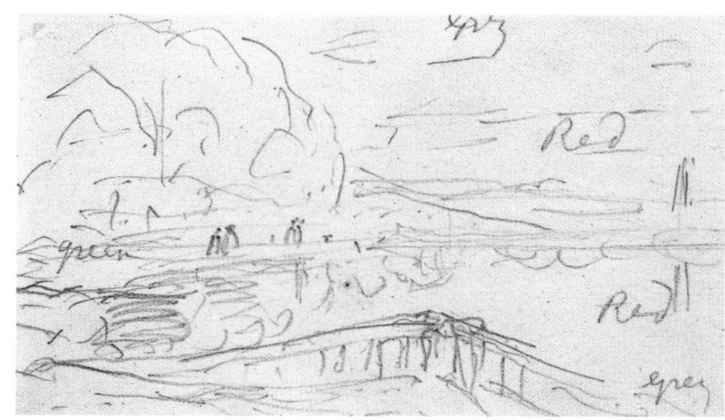

40. Annotated Sketch for 33
Pencil 3¼ x 5½ ins *(Ref. D3)*
Verso: Tree Sketch

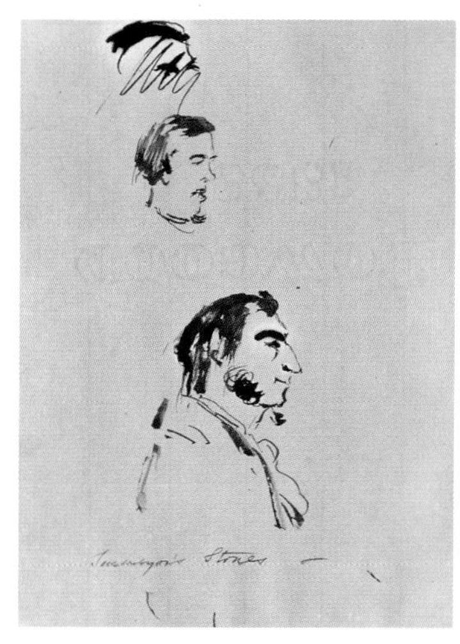

41. Surveyor's Stones
Pen and ink 8½ x 6½ ins
Inscribed *Surveyor's Stones*
Stones were placed as markers from which measurements were taken, hence the nickname for a surveyor's assistant. There were four qualified surveyors in Woodbridge in Churchyard's day.

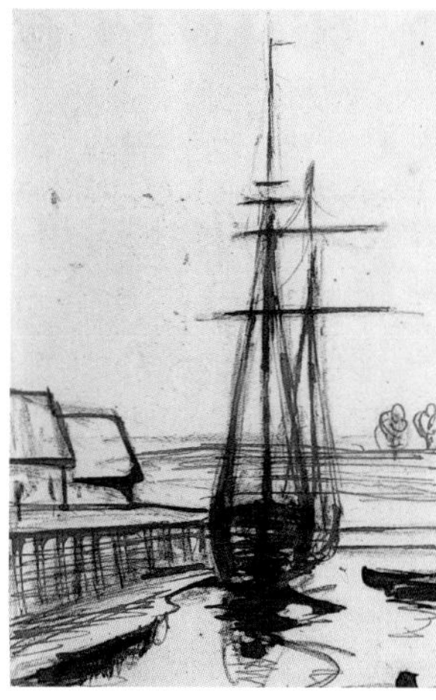

42. Moored Boat
Pen and ink 7 x 4½ ins
(Ref. D3)

43. Distant View of Woodbridge
Black chalk 3¼ x 4½ ins
(Ref. E3)

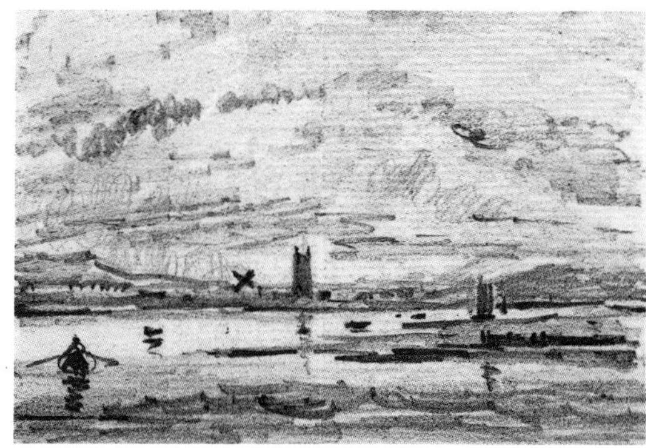

J.C. One such, for instance, slipped into the Paul Mellon Collection (number 98 in Basil Taylor's 1963 catalogue). The unfortunate Tom was thus waylaid at both ends, on the one hand robbed of his best and, on the other, stuffed with the well-meaning but less compelling efforts of his daughters. He became, moreover, a convenient receptacle for a wide range of unidentified East Anglian paintings of the mid-19th century.

Yet despite these many obstacles a solid basis of recognition began to emerge and by the mid-1960s Churchyard was widely acknowledged as one of the great British masters of the 19th century, the heir to Constable and Crome and an important link between them and Wilson Steer. His work was also finding its way to major public and private collections: to the Tate Gallery, the British Museum, the Victoria and Albert, the Ashmolean, the Fitzwilliam, the Norwich Castle Museum and Christchurch Mansion, Ipswich. An excellent monograph by Denis Thomas appeared in 1965.

Like all the great landscapists, Churchyard knew how to create an idyll from the simplest of scenes. On the surface all is lightness of touch, delicate observation and attention to detail, yet behind these lies a burning intensity tempered only by a natural reserve and the experience of a lifetime. Everything is freshly seen, as though the artist had chanced upon it for the first time. Repetition and easy formulas are sedulously avoided. Churchyard was an inspired colourist, finding unexpected combinations and converting them into the prevailing mood and *leitmotif* of his pictures. Nothing is fluffed, muddied or over-simplified; the eye wanders contentedly over every inch of the landscape, stretching away into the distance, unhindered by any meretricious irrelevance. Figures and animals are embedded in

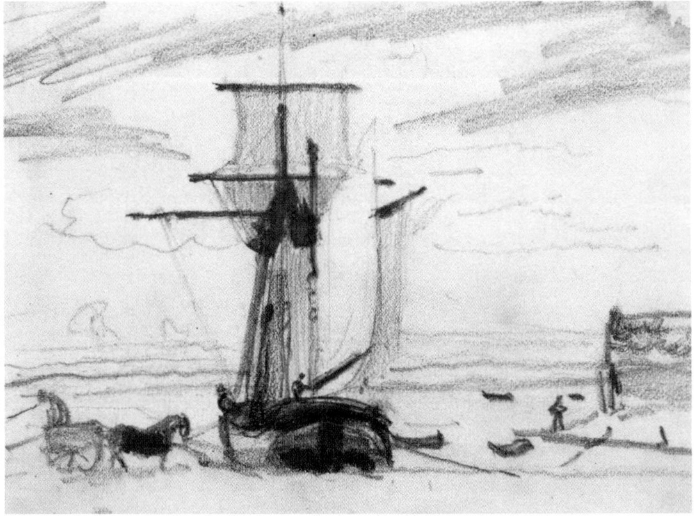

44. Ship in Dock, Woodbridge
Black chalk 4 x 5 ins

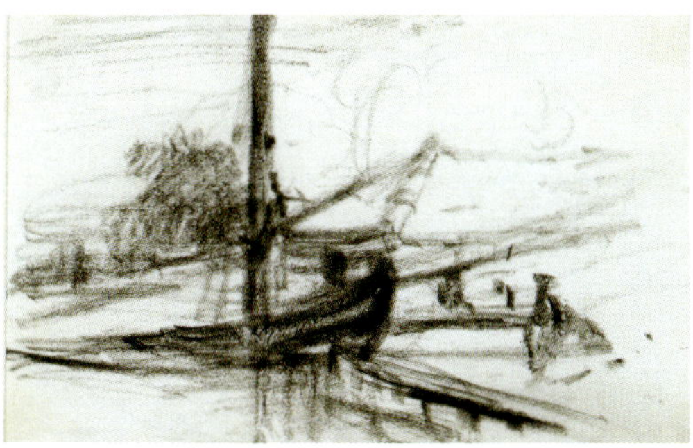

45. Ship at Anchor
Black chalk 2¼ x 3½ ins

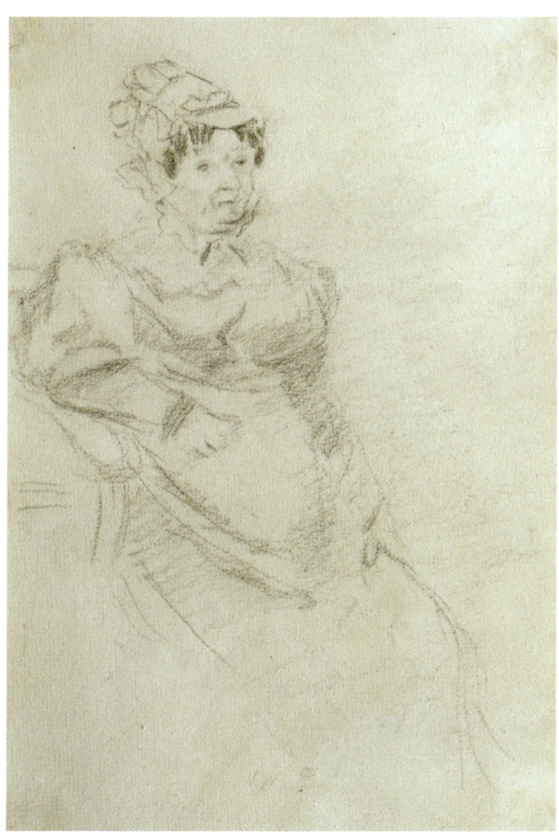

46. The Artist's Wife, Harriet
Pencil 8¼ x 5½ ins

the landscape as though they had never been anywhere else. The scale is often small and magnification reveals the jewel-like quality of the painting and the consummate mastery of his hand. The poetry is in the painting.

His early work, that which can be traced to the 1830s, is relatively typical of the period, often resembling that of his close contemporary Norwich School painters, such as James Stark (1794-1859). It was only later, and especially after 1850, that his style became wholly personal and independent. The watercolours and drawings in this exhibition belong almost exclusively to this later period. The only certain example of his early style is the oil painting number 82, which is dated 1833.

Every picture included in this exhibition was acquired at the seminal sale of 1927. The oil paintings establish their authenticity by TC's inscription of a daughter's name on the back, respectively Bessie Churchyard (No. 29) and the other three Emma Churchyard (Nos. 30, 82 and 83). What is all but unique, however, is the fact that 90 of the watercolours and drawings shown in the exhibition have been directly removed from one of the guard-books given to a daughter, in this case Emma, by her father. With only one exception, a guard-book sold in Nottingham in 1995, no other album directly bequeathed by TC is known to have escaped unrecorded dispersal. As a result these 90 watercolours and drawings have a rare and precious status in the oeuvre currently attributed to the master.

The other 66 watercolours and drawings derive from an album compiled by Harriet. In this case their attribution to Thomas is based on style. They are plainly beyond the reach of Laura, Anna and Harriet herself. Some of the other contents of the album (not included in this catalogue), however, are believed to be Anna's work.

The Countryside around Woodbridge

Provenance of the watercolours and drawings in this section:

Nos. 47-81 The Emma Churchyard Album, then to Elizabeth (Bessie) Churchyard and then to Harriet Churchyard, then to Agnes Shaw (née Airy) and thence by descent.

Nos. 82-83 As catalogued.

Nos. 84-109 The Harriet Churchyard Album, then to Agnes Shaw (née Airy) and thence by descent.

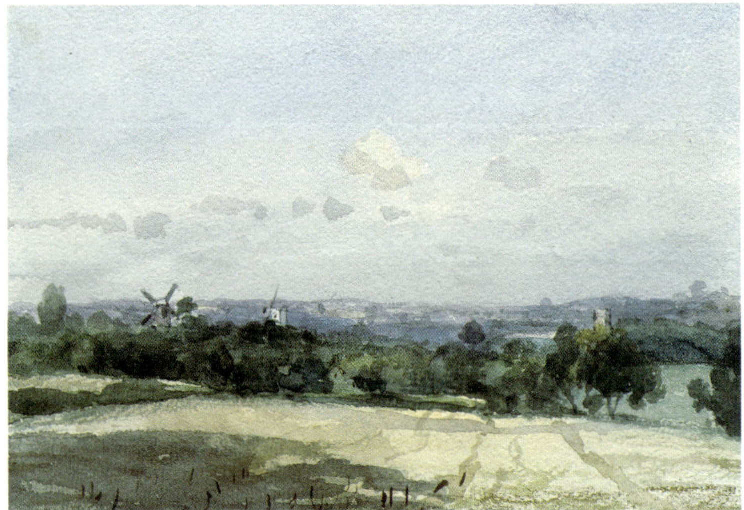

47. Cornfield near Hasketon
Watercolour 4¾ x 6¾ ins *(Ref. B1)*
Inscribed *Hasketon*

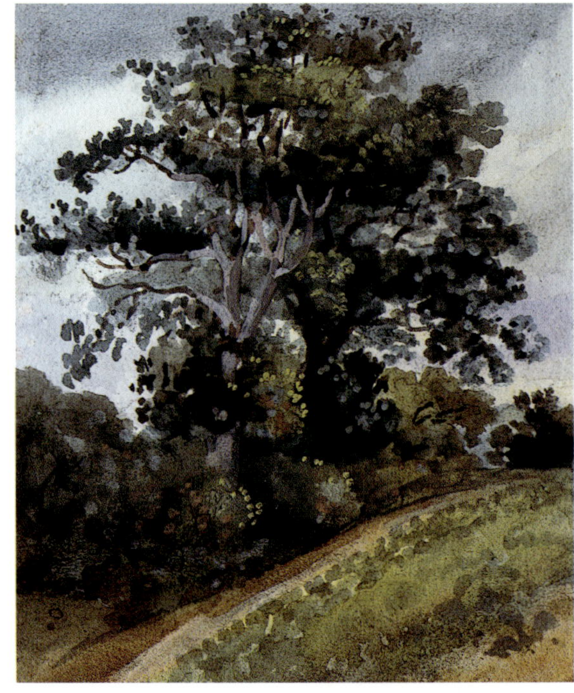

48. Trees on a Hillside
Watercolour 4¾ x 3¾ ins

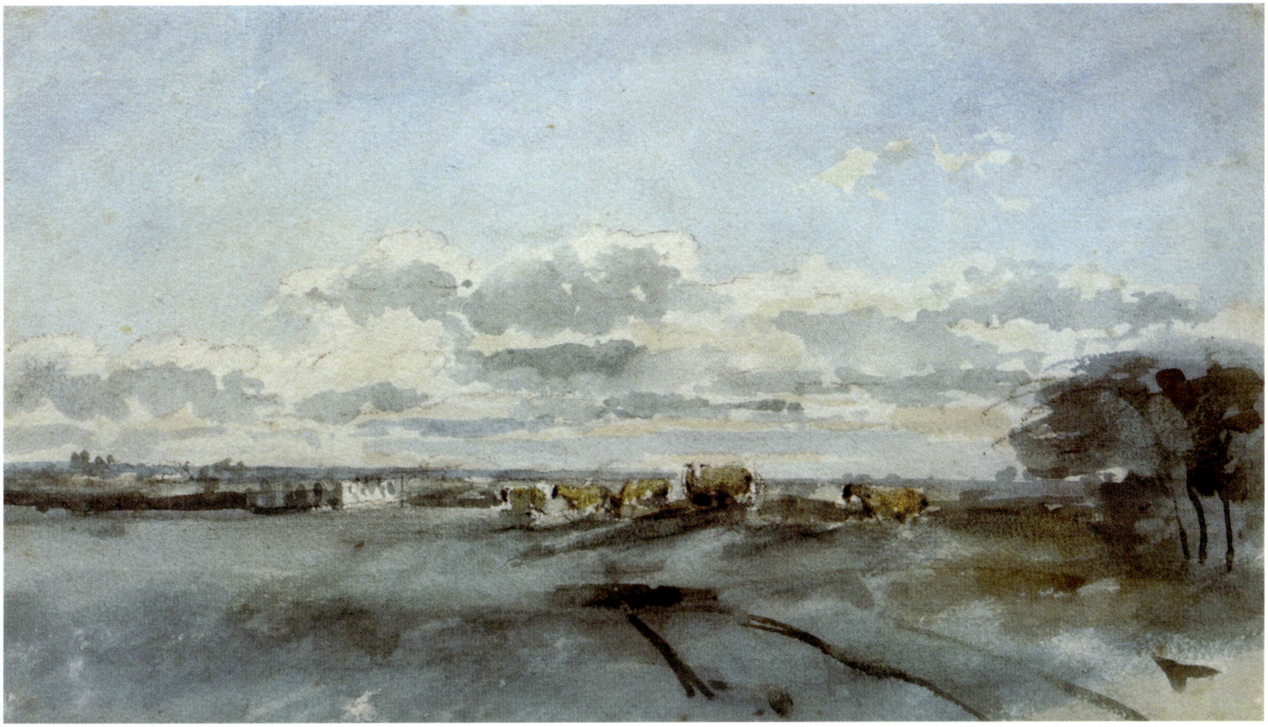

49. Near Seckford Hall
Watercolour 6½ x 11 ins
Inscribed *Near Seckford Hall*
This Elizabethan Mansion a mile west of Woodbridge is now a hotel. It was built by Thomas Seckford, a lawyer, a member of parliament and a major benefactor. The town is greatly indebted to him. School, hospital, library and almshouses all owe their existence to his charitable giving. It was also he who built the Shire Hall on Market Hill and Woodbridge Abbey near St Mary's Church. As it happens the Churchyard daughters were much indebted to the Seckford Charity after their father's death in 1865. *(Ref. D2)*

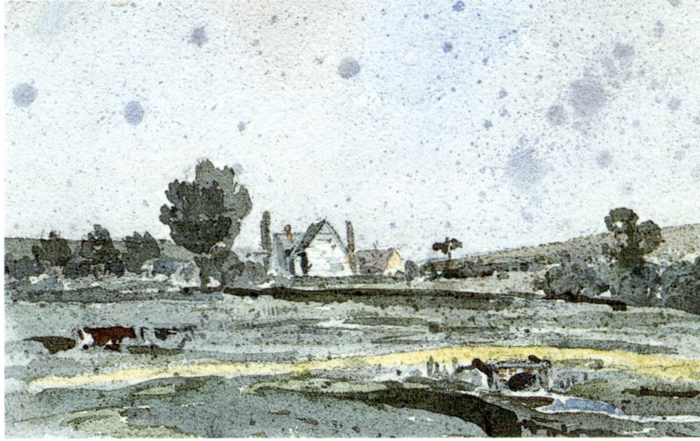

50. Bromeswell Common
Watercolour 5¼ x 7½ ins *(Ref. B5)*
Inscribed *Bromeswell Common*

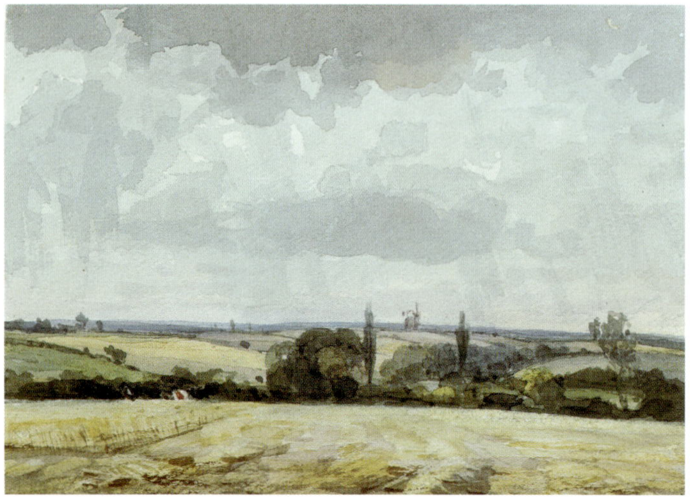

51. Across the Fields Towards Woodbridge
Watercolour 5¾ x 7¾ ins
Inscribed *at Woodbridge*
The sails of Buttrum's Windmill can be seen on the horizon. *(Ref. C2)*

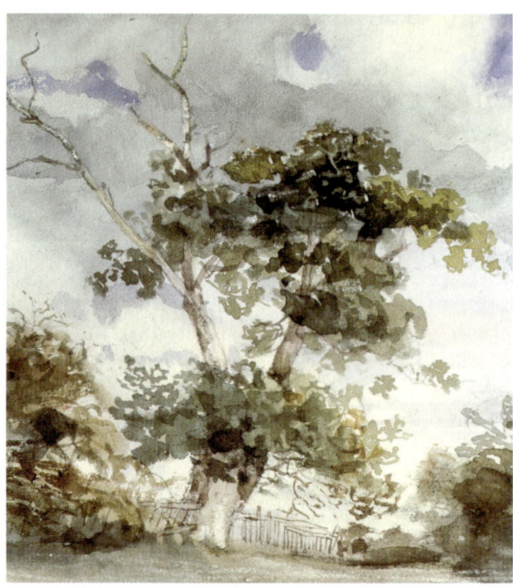

53. Tree Astride a Fence
Watercolour 6½ x 5½ ins

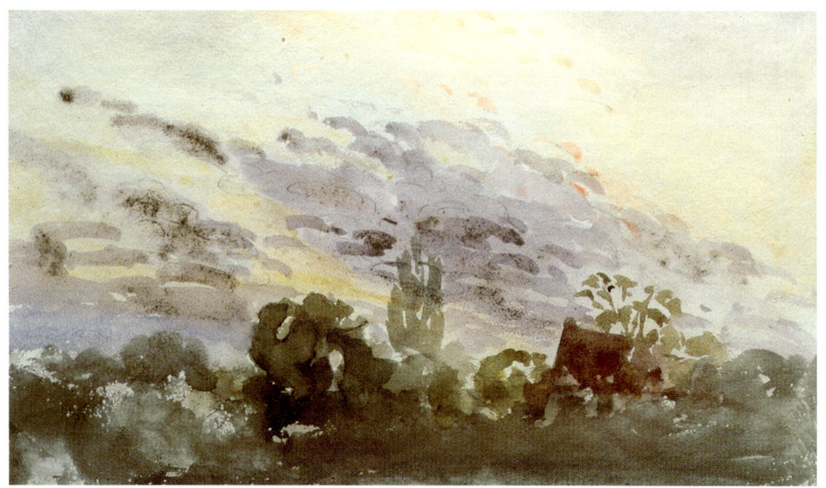

52. A Freckled Sky, Evening
Watercolour 5¼ x 8¾ ins

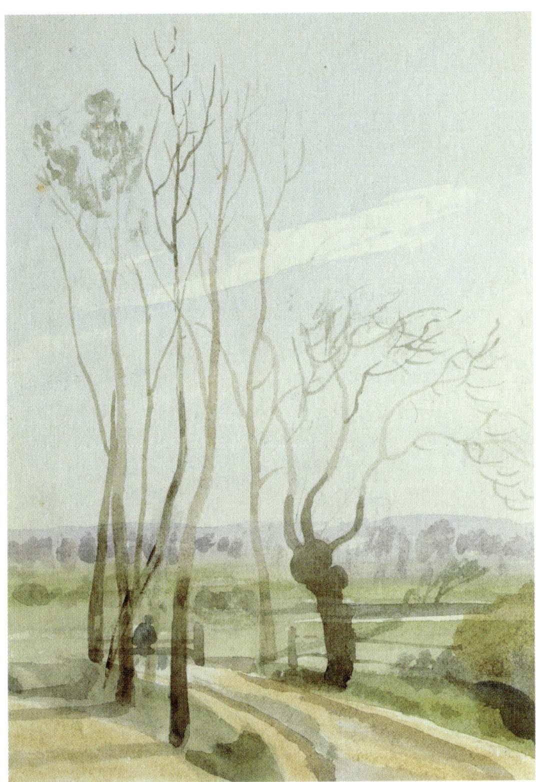

54. Figure on a Path
Watercolour 8 x 5¼ ins

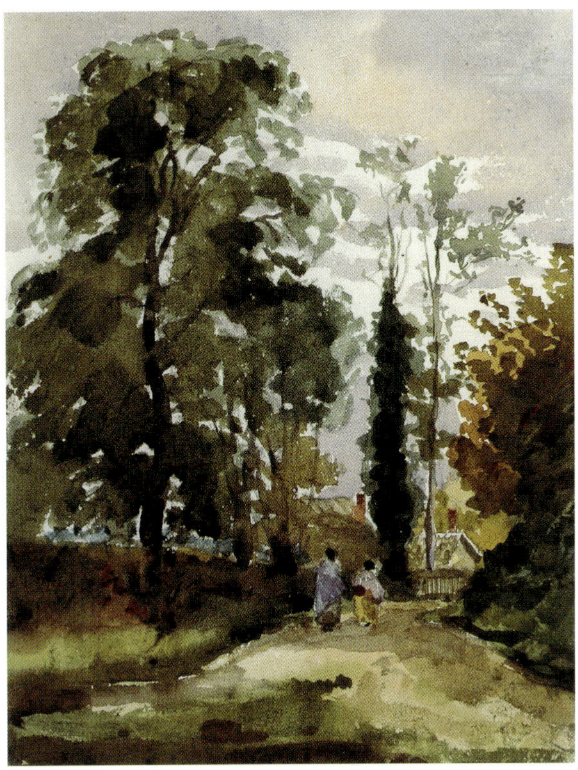

56. On The Way Home
Watercolour 7¾ x 5¾ ins *(Ref. B4)*
Probably at Melton, two miles north of Woodbridge.

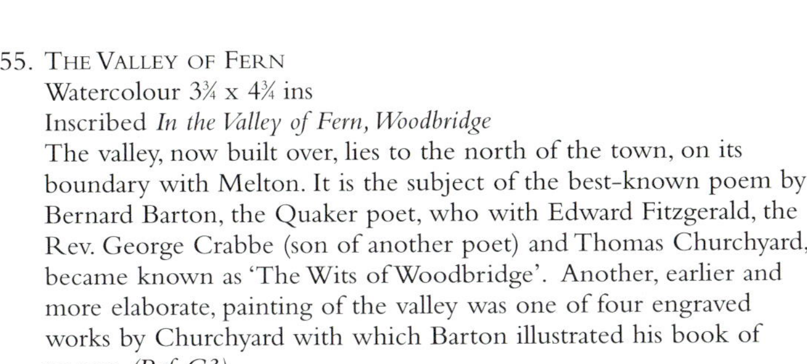

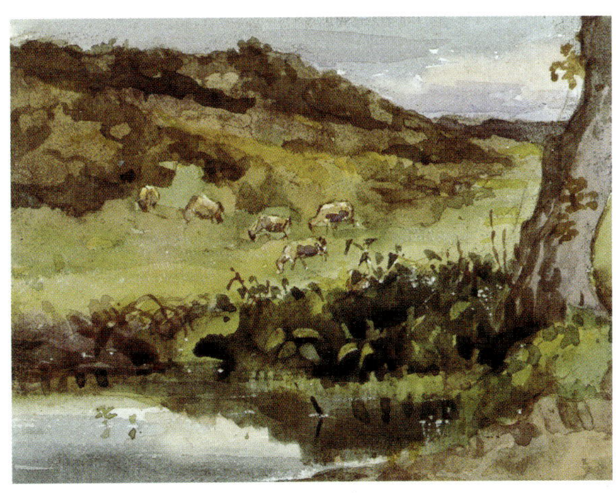

55. The Valley of Fern
Watercolour 3¾ x 4¾ ins
Inscribed *In the Valley of Fern, Woodbridge*
The valley, now built over, lies to the north of the town, on its boundary with Melton. It is the subject of the best-known poem by Bernard Barton, the Quaker poet, who with Edward Fitzgerald, the Rev. George Crabbe (son of another poet) and Thomas Churchyard, became known as 'The Wits of Woodbridge'. Another, earlier and more elaborate, painting of the valley was one of four engraved works by Churchyard with which Barton illustrated his book of poems. *(Ref. C3)*

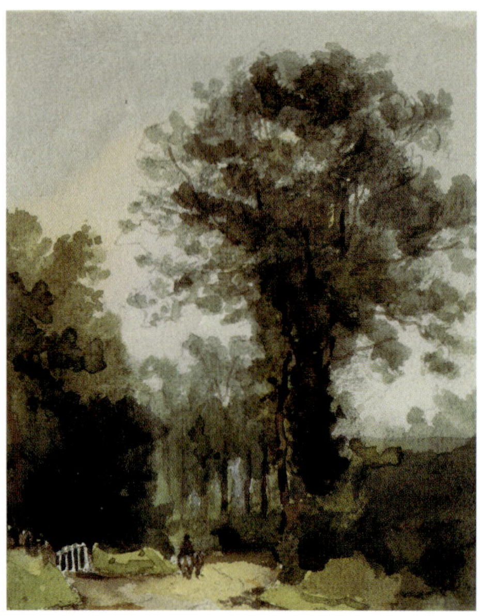

57. Lawyer Wood's Lane, Melton
Watercolour 4¾ x 3¾ ins
Inscribed *at Woodbridge*
On the boundary between Woodbridge and Melton and now known as Wood's Lane. Melton was Churchyard's birthplace and his home for much of his life. *(Ref. C3)*

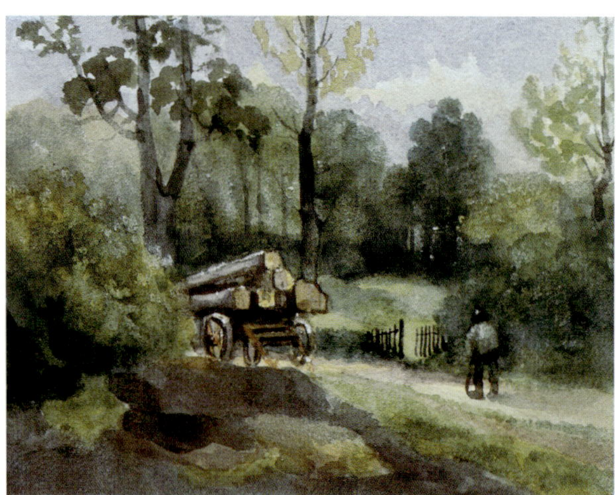

58. Timber Waggon at Melton
Watercolour 3¾ x 4¾ ins *(Ref. B4)*
Inscribed *at Melton*

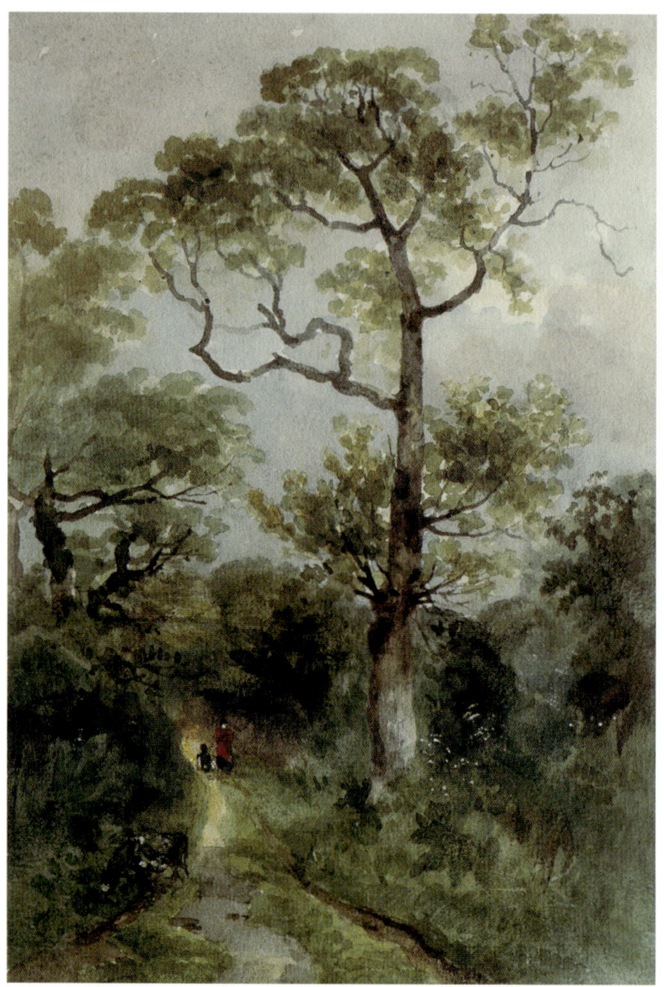

59. Wooded Path near Martlesham
Watercolour 9 x 6 ins *(Ref. E2)*
Inscribed *at Martlesham*

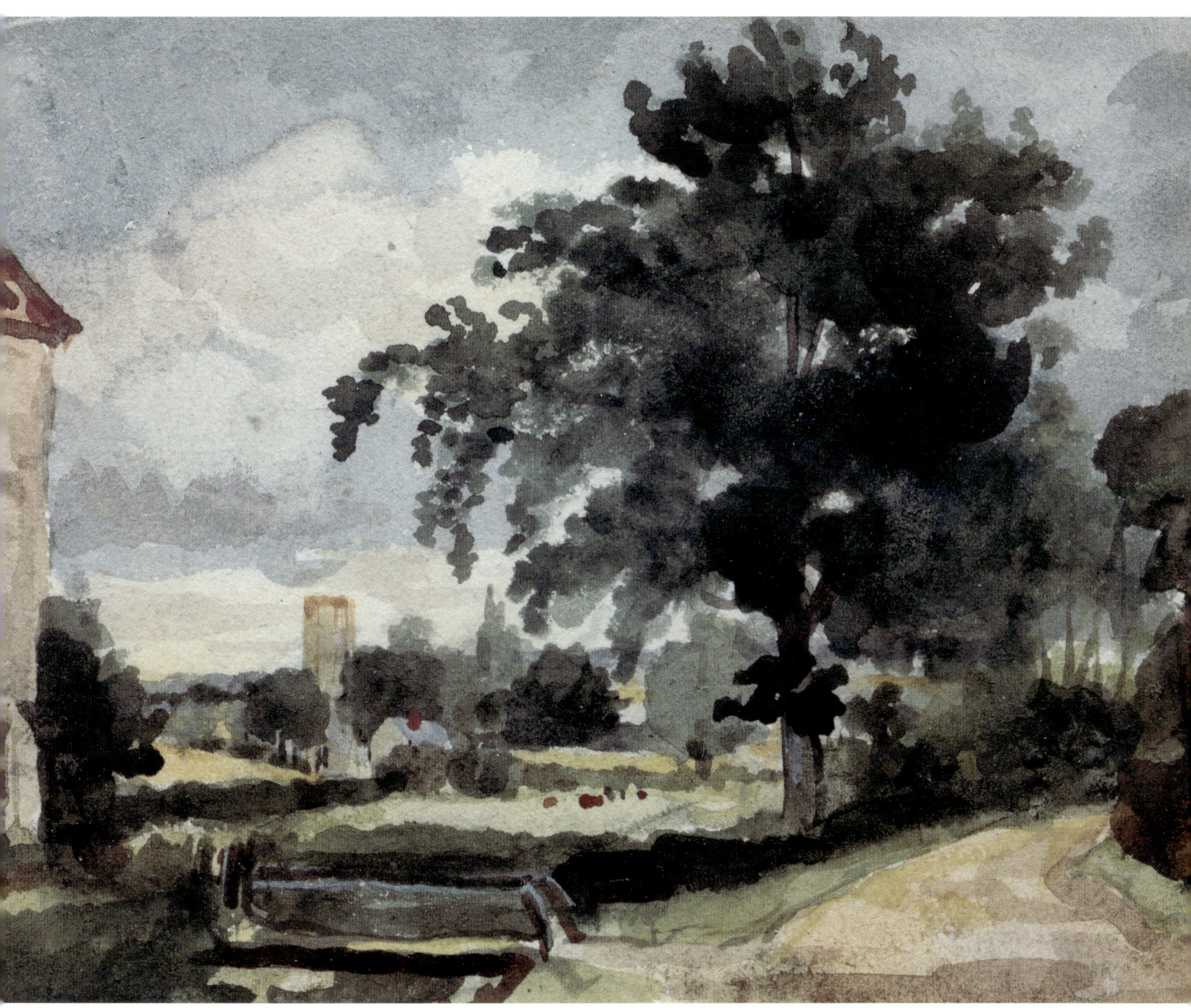

60. Hasketon
Watercolour 3¾ x 4¾ ins *(Ref. B1)*
Inscribed *at Hasketon*

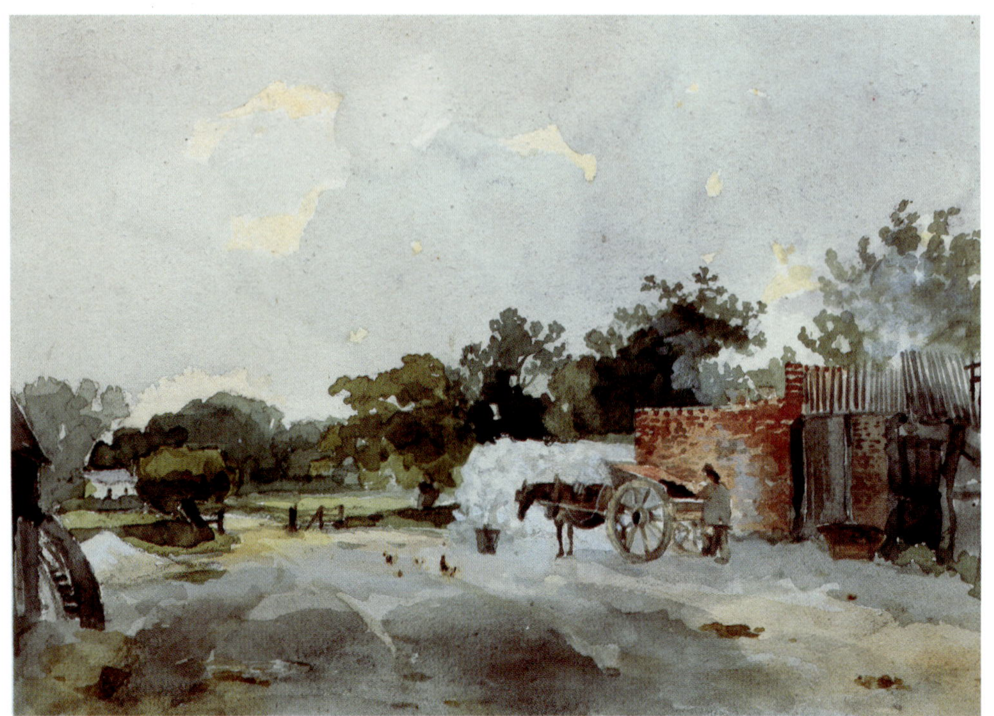

61. Builders' Merchant at Melton
Watercolour 5¾ x 7¾ ins
Inscribed *at Melton*
William Cook was a brick and tile maker near Wilford Bridge at Melton. The waterwheel – just showing left – suggests this identification. *(Ref. C4)*

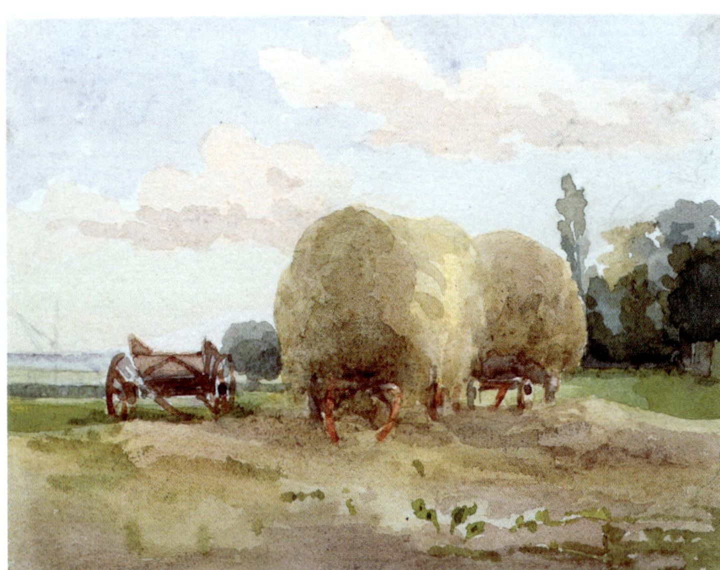

62. Carting Hay
Watercolour 3¾ x 4¾ ins

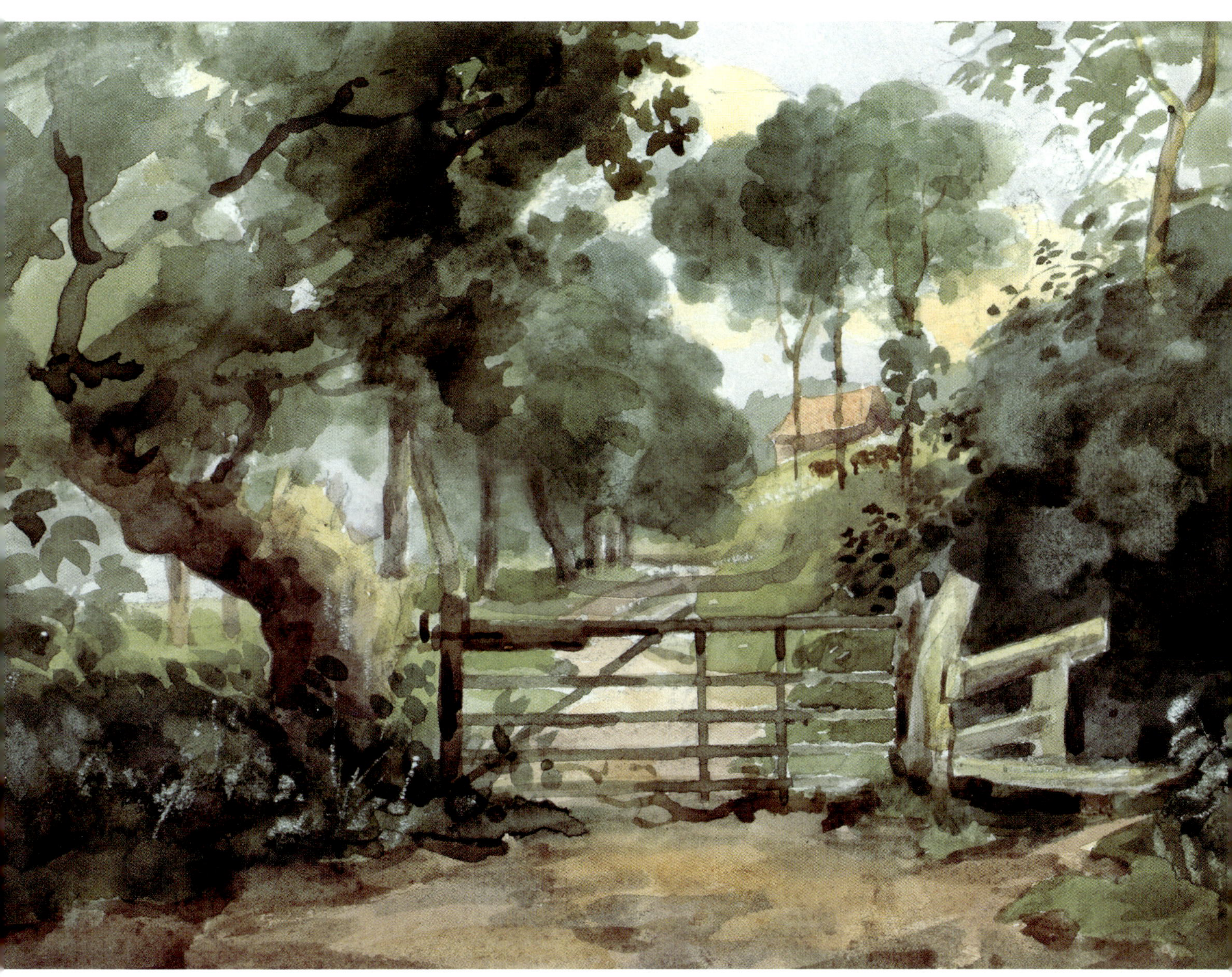

63. Country Path with Gate *(Front cover – detail)*
Watercolour 5¾ x 7¾ ins
Probably near Martlesham. *(Ref. E2)*

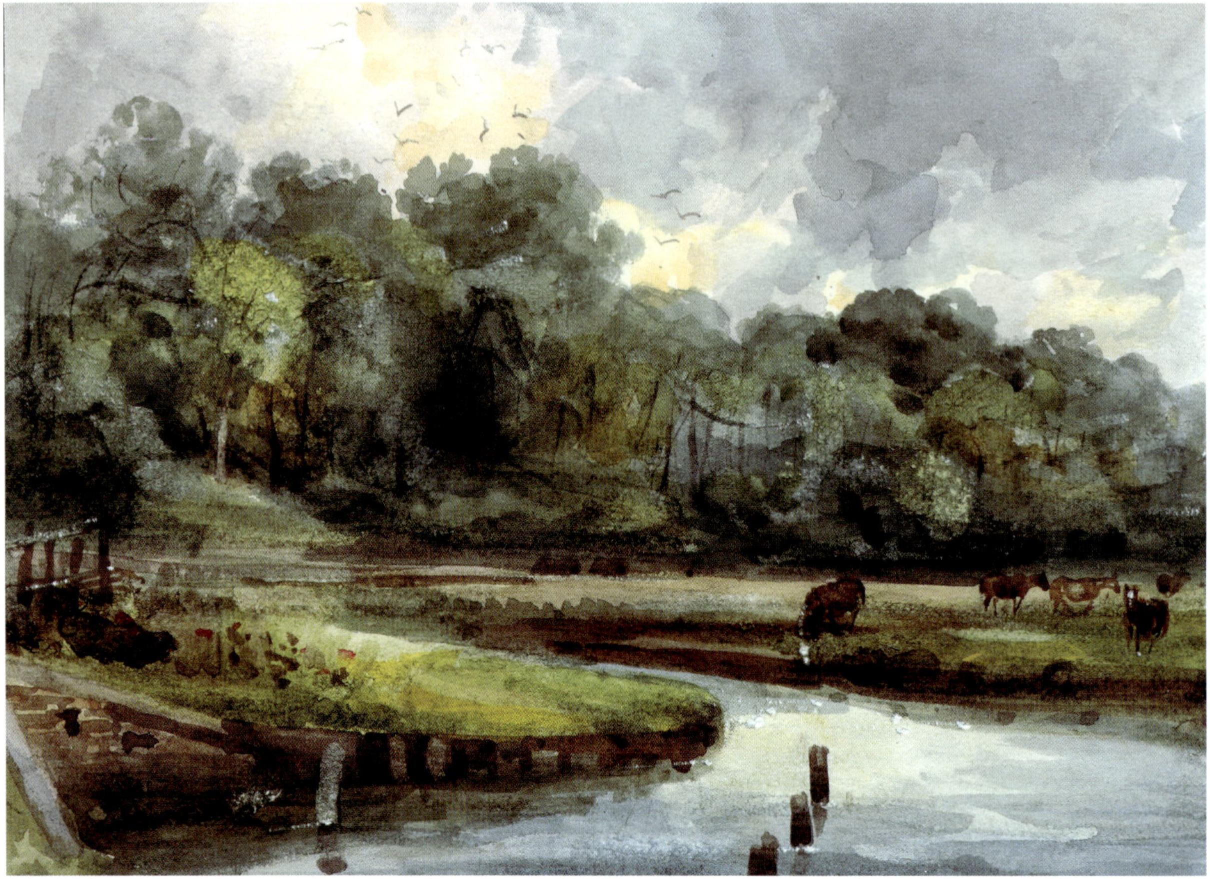

64. Horses Grazing by a River
Watercolour 5¾ x 7¾ ins
Might be upper reaches of the Deben near Ufford. *(Ref. B5)*

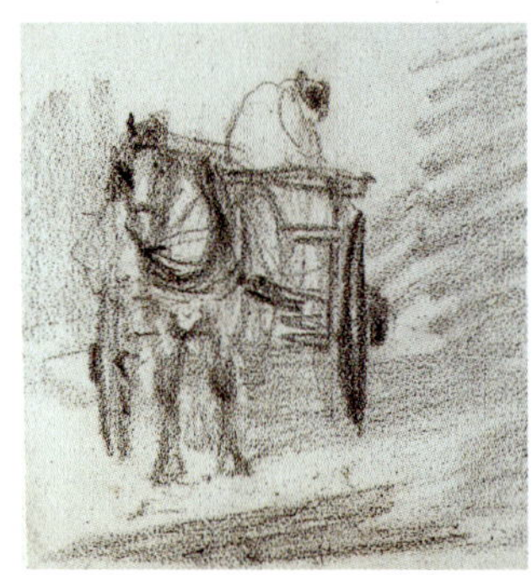

65. A Brief Halt
Black chalk 3½ x 2¾ ins

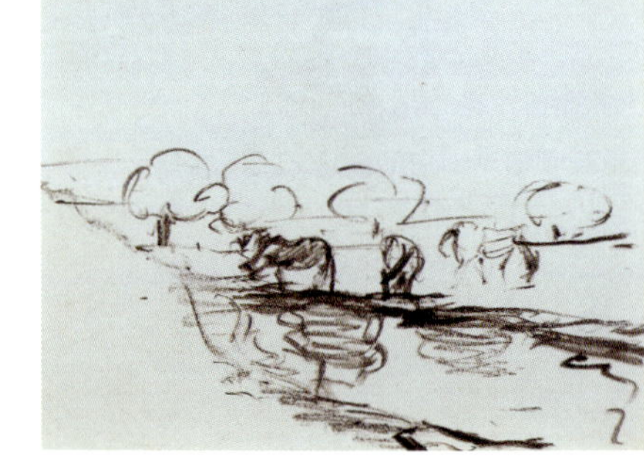

66. Horses beside a River
Black chalk 3½ x 4¼ ins

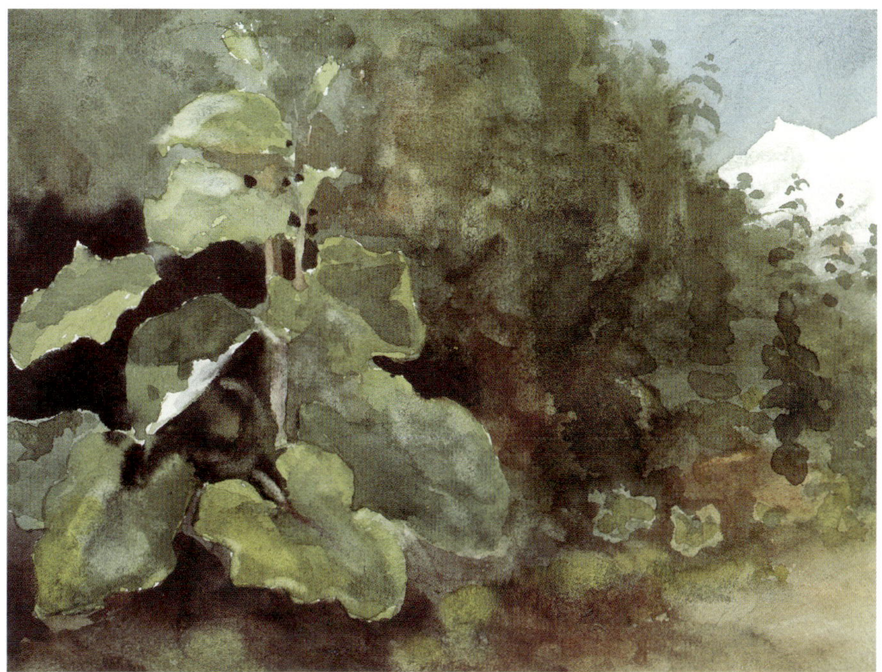

67. Study of Dock Leaves
Watercolour 5¾ x 7¾ ins

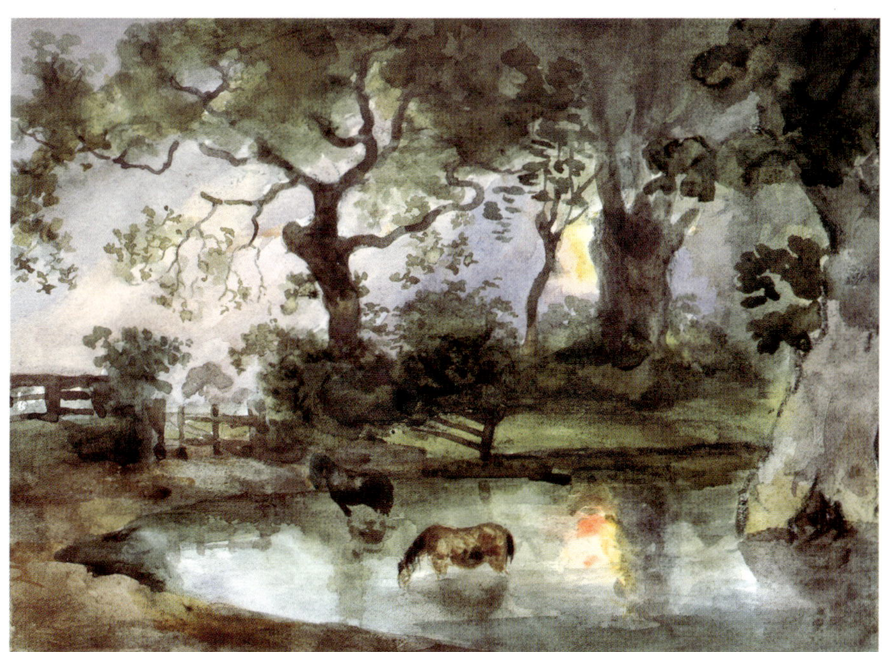

68. Horses Watering, Evening Storm
Watercolour 5¾ x 7¾ ins

69. Artist Sketching
Black chalk 3 x 5½ ins
There is no record of Churchyard ever having employed such a contraption, or anybody else for that matter, but it appears to have advantages for the plein-air addict.

70. Loaded Donkey Cart
Black chalk 3 x 4¾ ins

71. Cow at Rest
Pencil 2¾ x 4¼ ins

72. Two Carts on a Road
Pen and ink 3½ x 5¾ ins

73. Sketch of Horse Grazing
Watercolour 3¼ x 5 ins

74. Study of Horse-Cart with Dog
Watercolour 3½ x 4¾ ins

75. Study of Saddled Horse
Watercolour 2½ x 3¼ ins

76. Midday Rest
Black chalk 3½ x 4¼ ins

77. Willow Trees
Black chalk 3½ x 6 ins

78. Farm Scene
Black chalk 3½ x 6 ins

79. Rural Scene
Black chalk 2½ x 4¼ ins
For this elaborate drawing Churchyard used a sheet from an engagements calendar covering the week 14-20 September 1856. It seems he had no engagements that week! Earlier in the year he had successfully acted for the prosecution in the case of Dr Rigaud, the Ipswich headmaster who had severely and undeservedly flogged a boy of 14 ('twenty times on various parts of the body'). Why had the boy not attempted to exonerate himself? "Because the more the excuses the harder the hits", was Churchyard's reply. Dr Rigaud was obliged to look for another job and accepted a bishopric in the West Indies.

80. A Visit to the Stables
Black chalk 3 x 4½ ins

81. Donkeys
Black chalk 2 x 3¼ ins

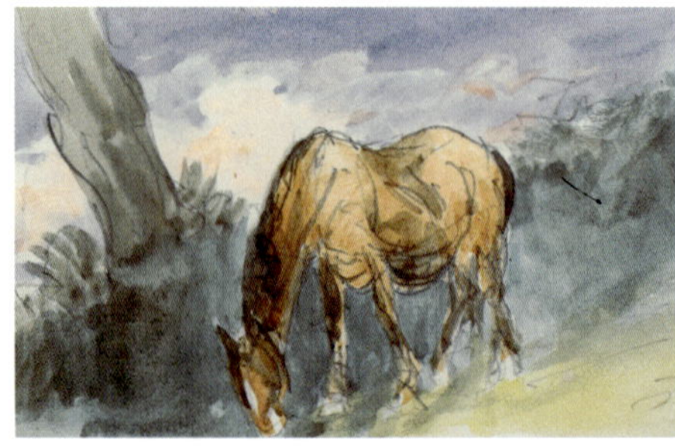
73.

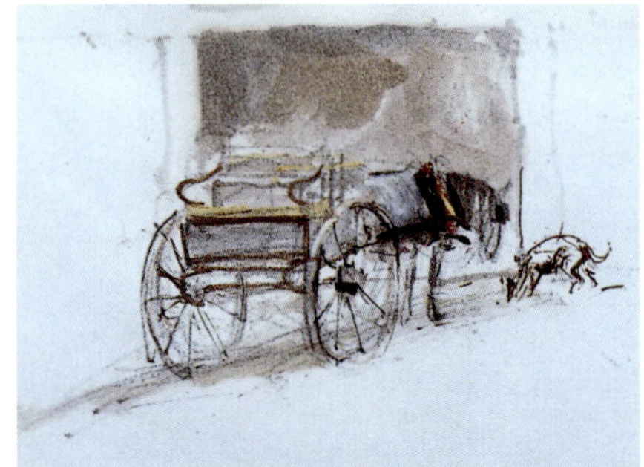
74.

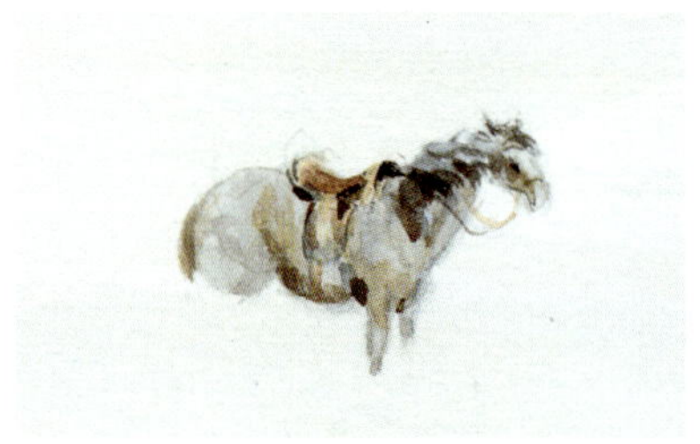
75.

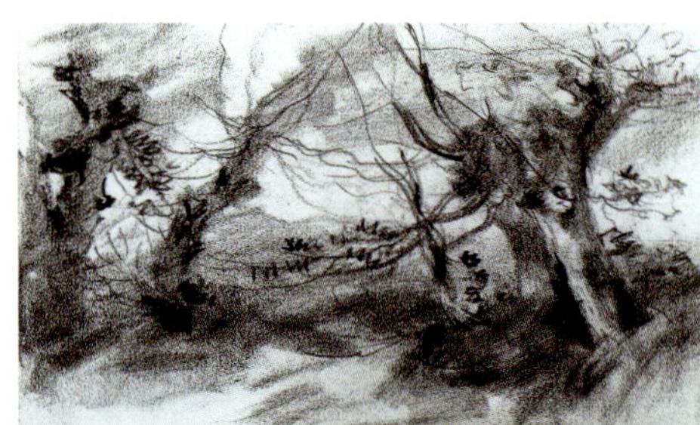
77.

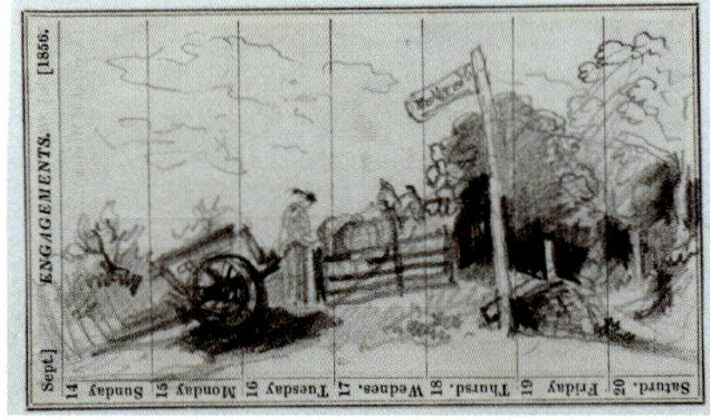

79.

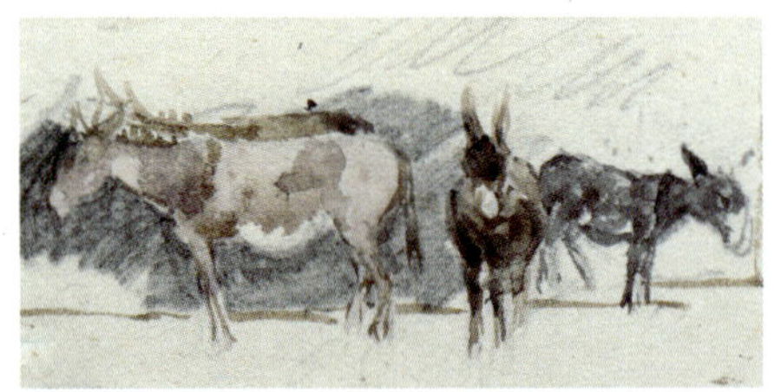
81.

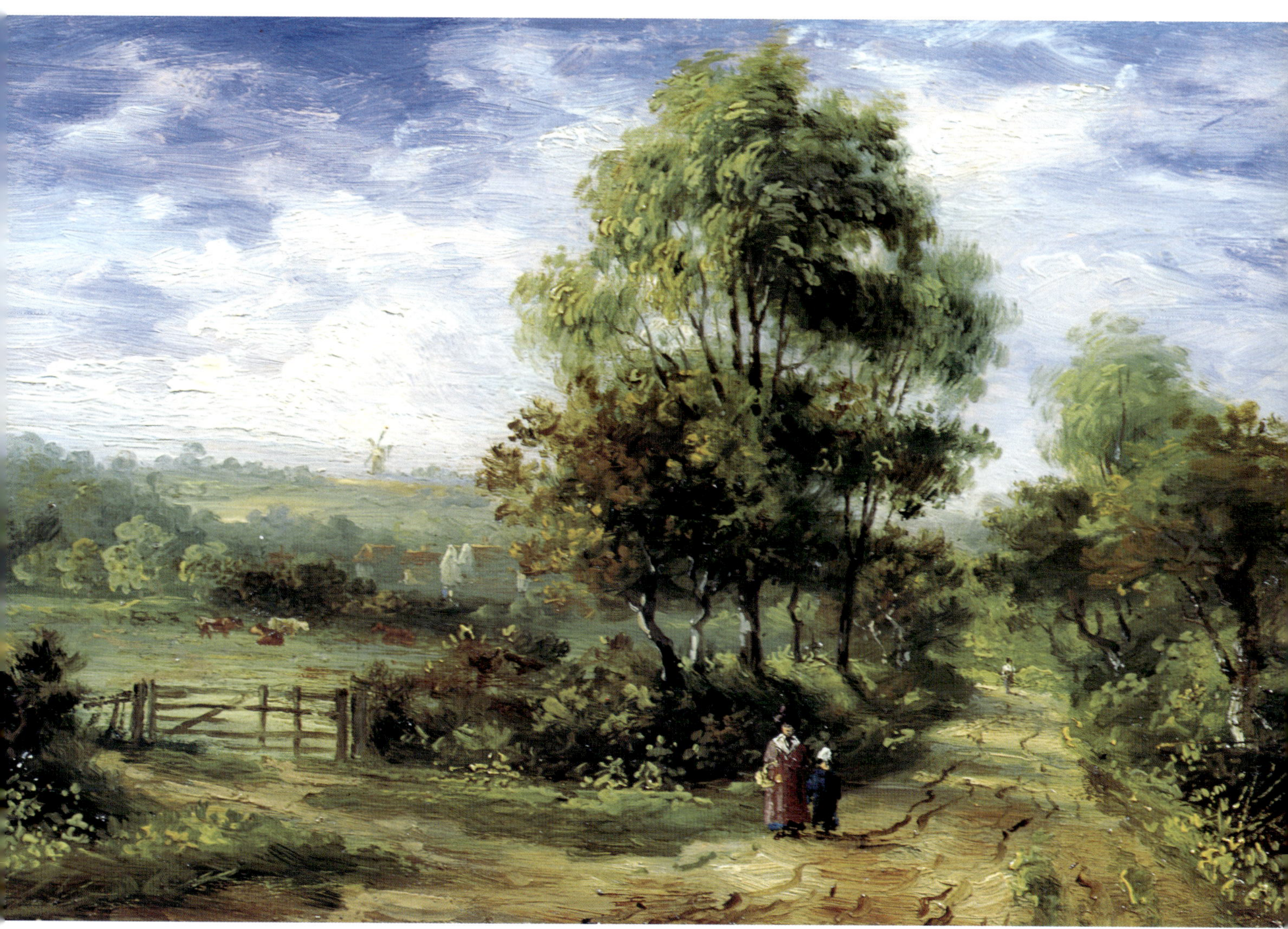

82. Lane at Martlesham, 1833
Oil on panel 5¾ x 8½ ins
Inscribed on reverse *Emma… Lane at Martlesham, 1833*
Provenance: Emma Churchyard, Anna Churchyard, Harriet Churchyard, her sale 1927 bought Gray family, Miss E.M. Gray, her sale Nottingham 1996.
Typical of the artist's early style. *(Ref. E2)*

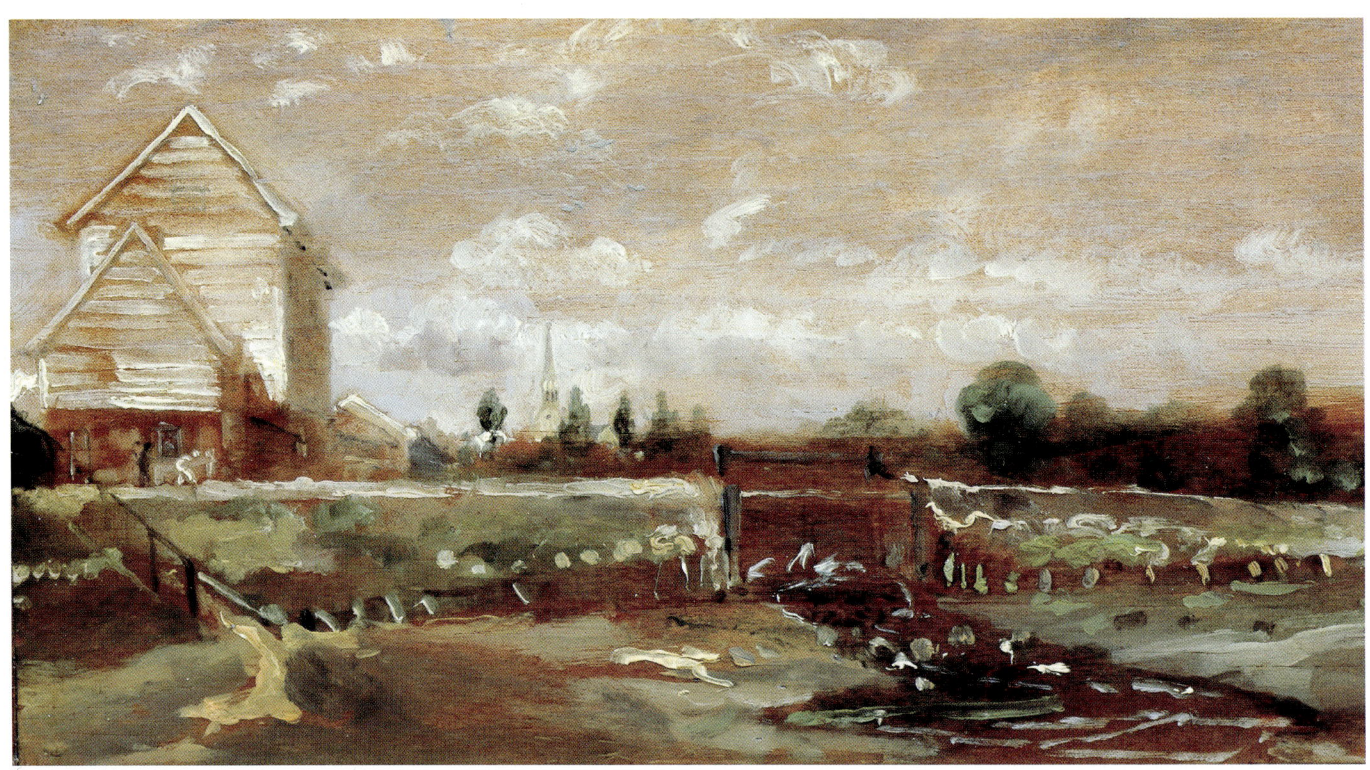

83. RACKHAM MILL
Oil on panel 5 x 9 ins
Inscribed *Emma* on reverse
Provenance: Emma Churchyard, Harriet Churchyard, Agnes Shaw (née Airy), thence by descent.
Wickham Market Church is seen in the distance.
(Ref. Coast Map F2)

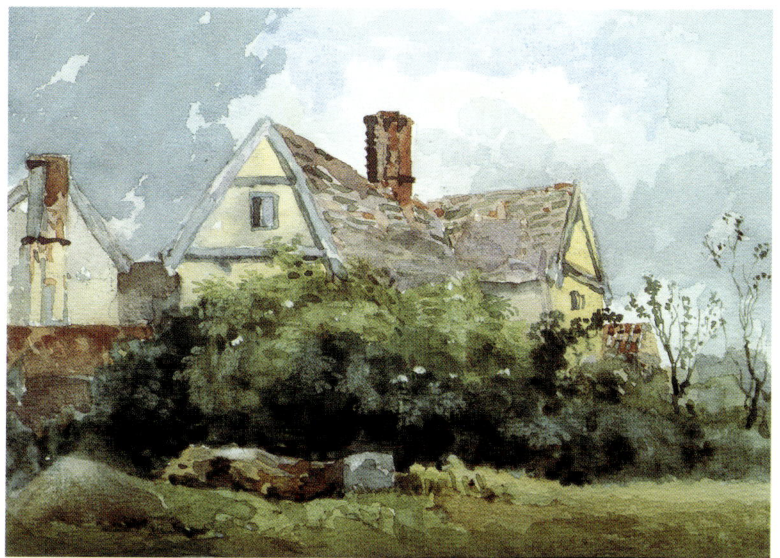

84. Gabled House behind a Hedge
Watercolour 5¾ x 7¾ ins

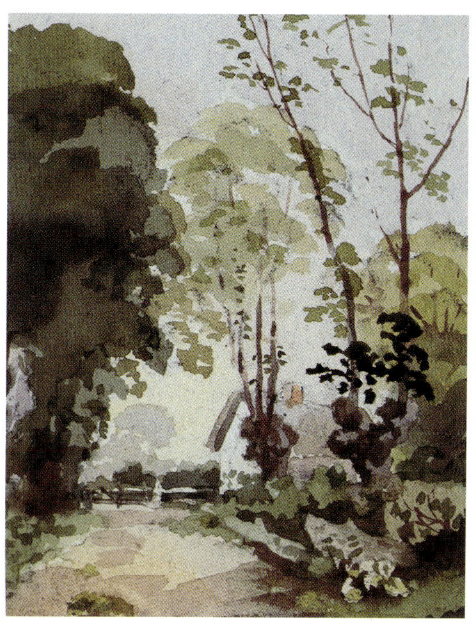

86. White Cottage among Trees
Watercolour 4¾ x 3¾ ins

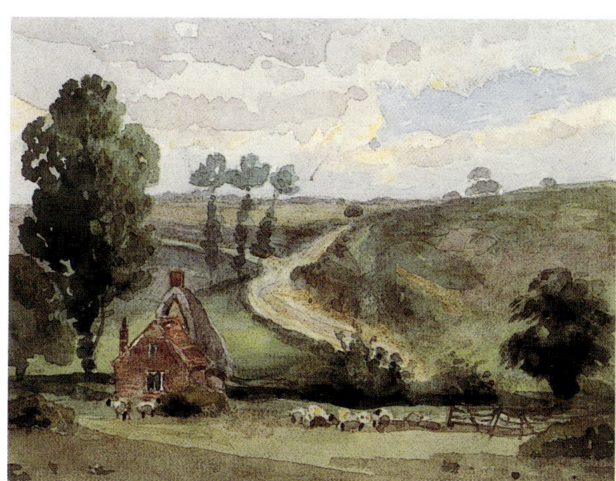

85. Shepherds Cottage, Bromeswell
Watercolour 3¾ x 4¾ ins
Close to the Deben, just over Wilford Bridge. *(Ref. C4)*

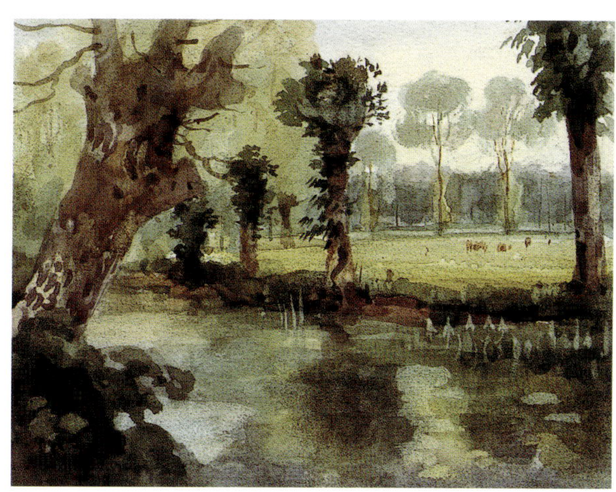

87. Water Meadows, Ufford
Watercolour 3¾ x 4¾ ins
Beside the upper reaches of the Deben. *(Ref. B5)*

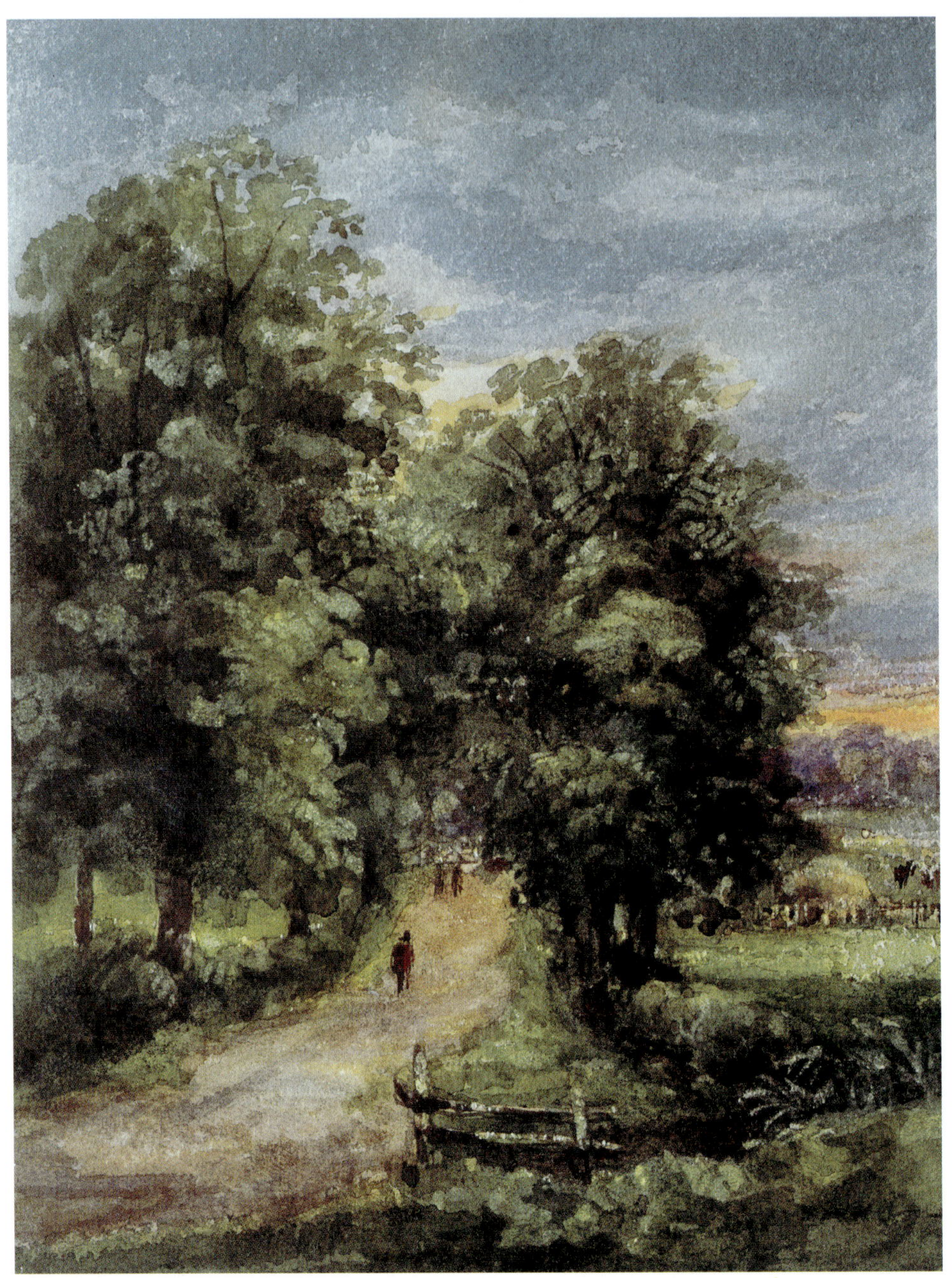

88. Figures on a Wooded Lane
Watercolour 7¾ x 5¾ ins
Possibly at Martlesham. *(Ref. E2)*

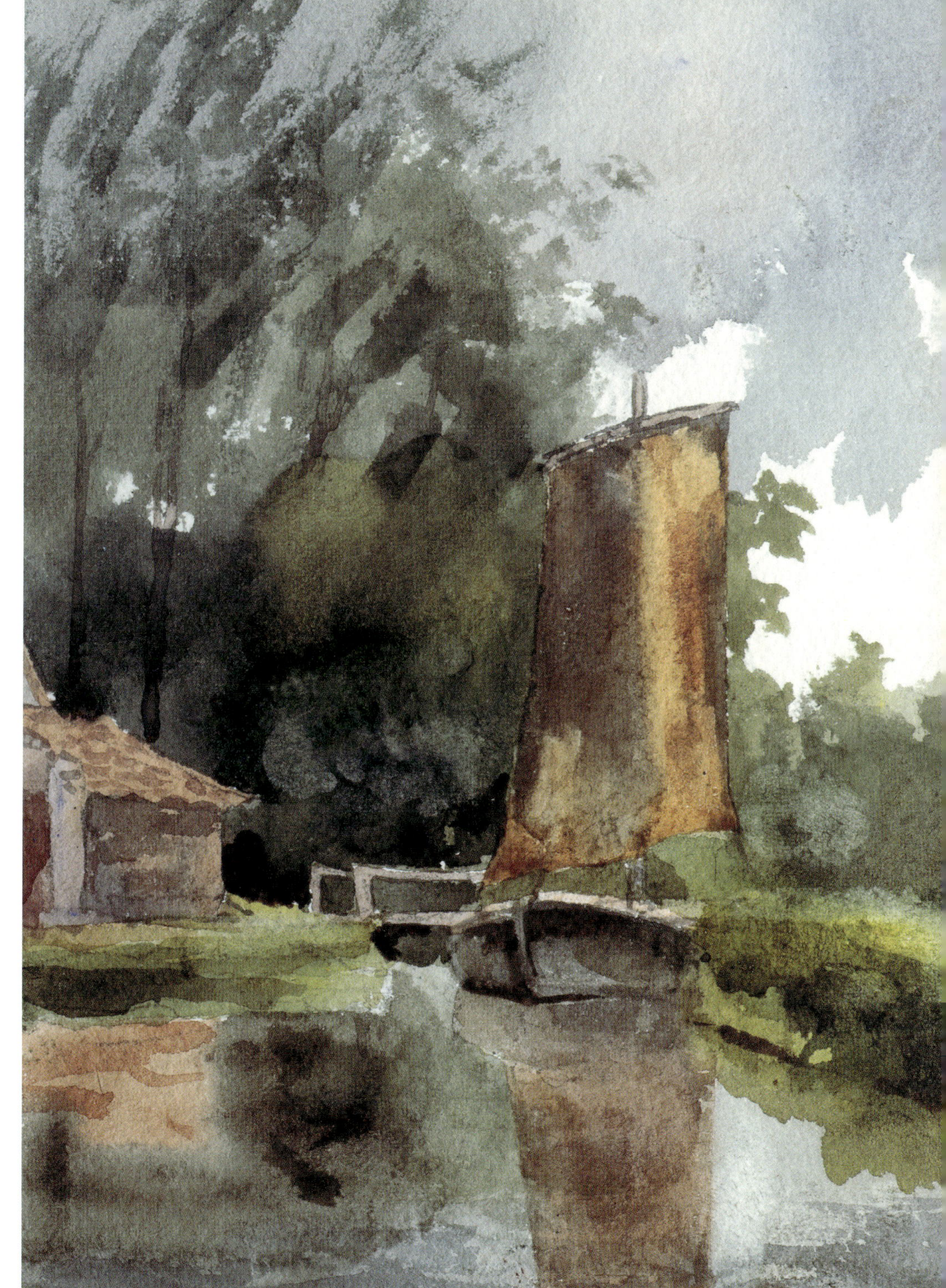

89. Moored Boat with Brown Sail
Watercolour 6¾ x 4¾ ins
Again the upper Deben.
(Ref. E2)

90. Farm Cart
Watercolour 4¼ x 5½ ins

91. Figure at the Stable Door
Black chalk 3½ x 4½ ins

92. Study of Tree with House Beyond
Black chalk 5½ x 3¼ ins

93. Farm Sheds and Cart
Black chalk 3¼ x 5¼ ins

94. Waggon Drawn by Three Horses
Pen and ink, watercolour wash
3¼ x 5½ ins

95. Farmer in a Small Donkey Cart
Black chalk 3½ x 3½ ins

96. A Roadside Discussion
Black chalk 3¼ x 5½ ins

97. Master King of Clopton
Black chalk 5 x 4¼ ins
Inscribed with title
John King, recorded in 1855 as a farmer at Clopton, a village 4 miles NW of Woodbridge. Churchyard probably knew his father James, hence 'master' (despite John's elderly appearance!) Churchyard's eldest son Tom (1825-96) also farmed 72 acres at Clopton before leaving for America (a second time) in 1863. He subsequently settled in New Zealand. He was a genial character like his father. (Clopton is just west of A1.)
Verso: Studies of Five Heads of Local Dignitaries
Watercolour monochrome 5 x 4 ins

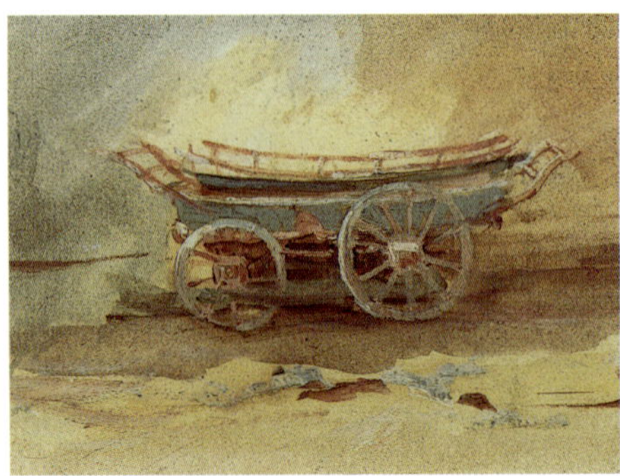

90.

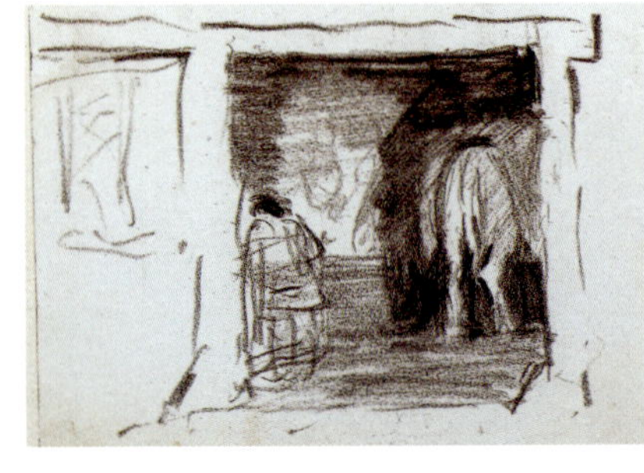

91.

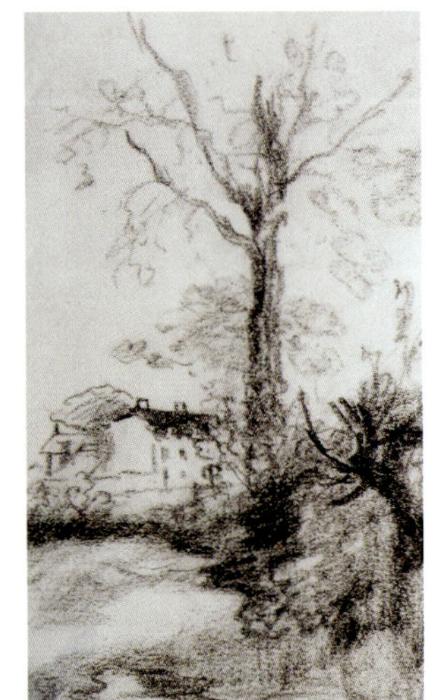

92.

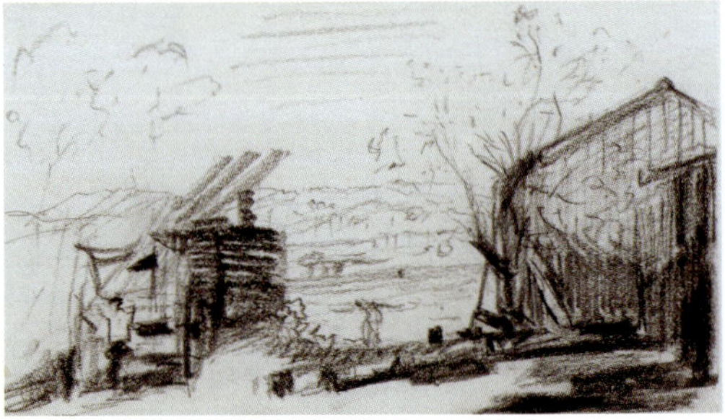

93.

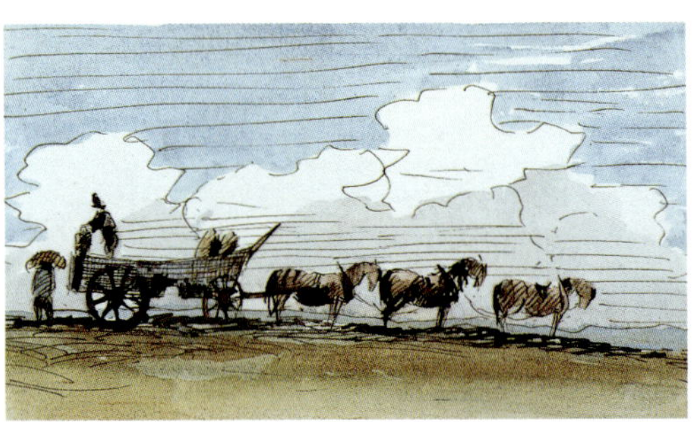

94.

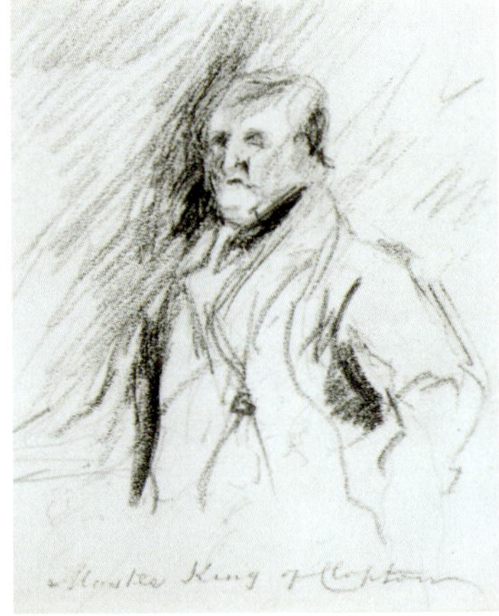

97.

98. Small Study of a Horse
Watercolour 1¾ x 2¾ ins

99. Horse Resting
Watercolour 2¼ x 4¼ ins

100. Study of a Horse and Cart
Black chalk 3 x 5½ ins

101. Oak Tree
Pen and ink 4 x 3 ins

102. Old Wilford Bridge, Melton
Black chalk 3¾ x 6 ins *(Ref. C4)*

103. Sketch of Cattle
Pencil 5 x 6 ins
Verso: Landscape with Sun
Pencil 5 x 6 ins

104. Hay Wagon
Pencil 3¼ x 5¾ ins

105. Landscape Sketch with Cottage
Pencil 6 x 7¾ ins

106. Postmill, Stiff Breeze
Black chalk 3¾ x 6 ins
Verso: Landscape with Figures

107. Farming Scene
Black chalk 4¼ x 5½ ins

108. The Valley of Fern
Pencil 3¾ x 5½ ins *(Ref. C3)*
See 55. When Barton wrote his poem in about 1820 he was already in despair at its despoliation: "Thou art changed, lovely spot!"

109. An Explosive Sky
Pen and sepia wash 4½ x 7¼ ins
Verso: Horses Head
Pen

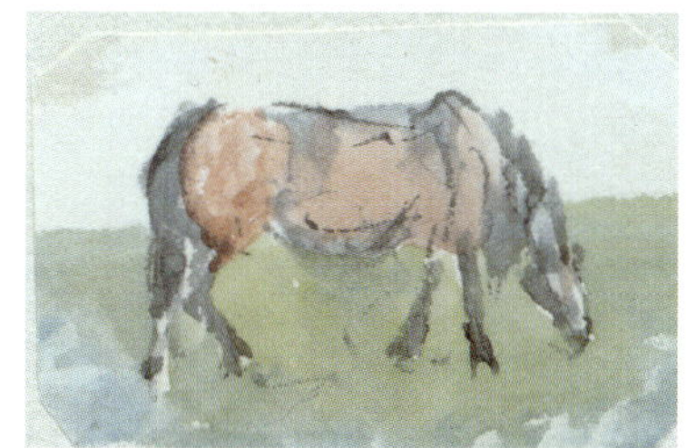

98.

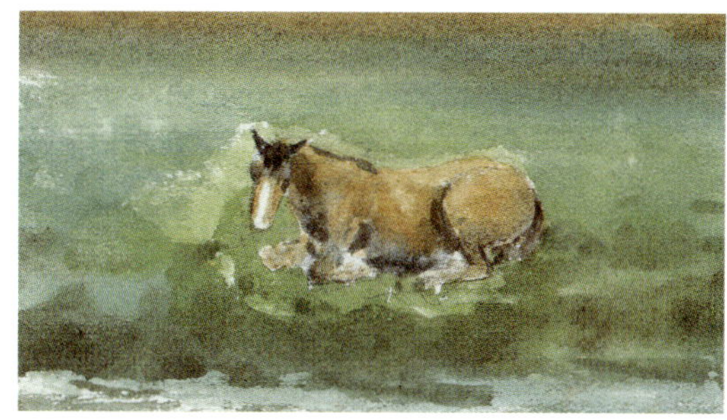

99.

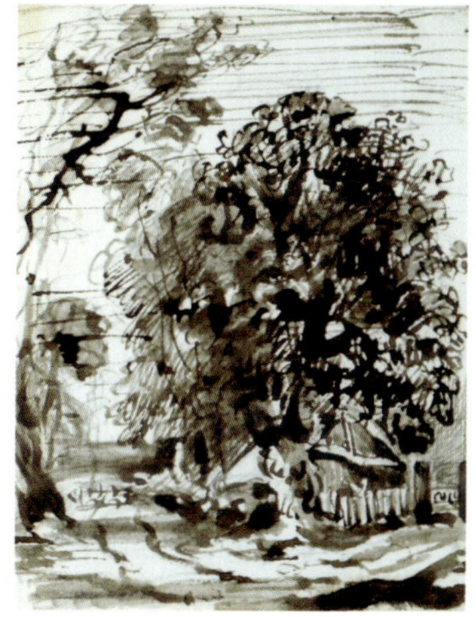

101.

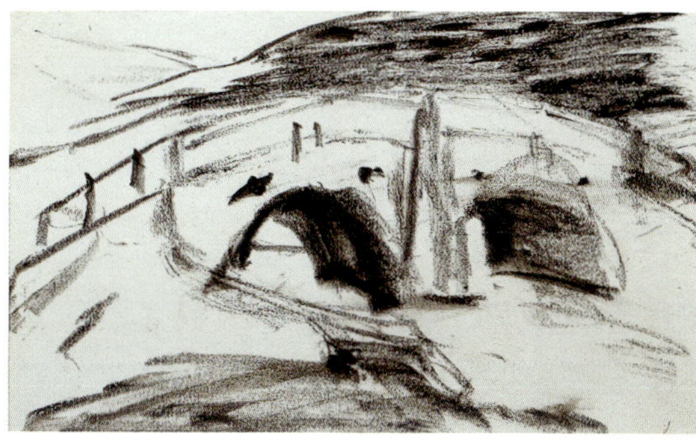

102.

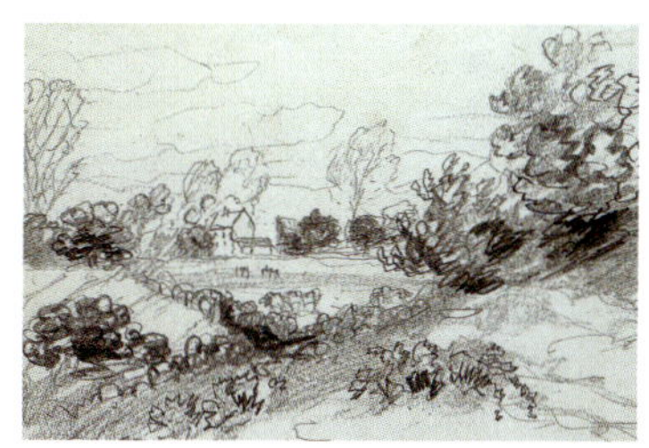

108.

109.

East Suffolk coast from Felixstowe to Great Yarmouth

Provenance of the watercolours and drawings in this section:
Each as catalogued. *Emma* = The Emma Churchyard Album, then to Elizabeth (Bessie) Churchyard, then to Harriet Churchyard, then to Agnes Shaw (née Airy) and thence by descent.
Harriet = The Harriet Churchyard Album, then to Agnes Shaw (née Airy) and thence by descent.

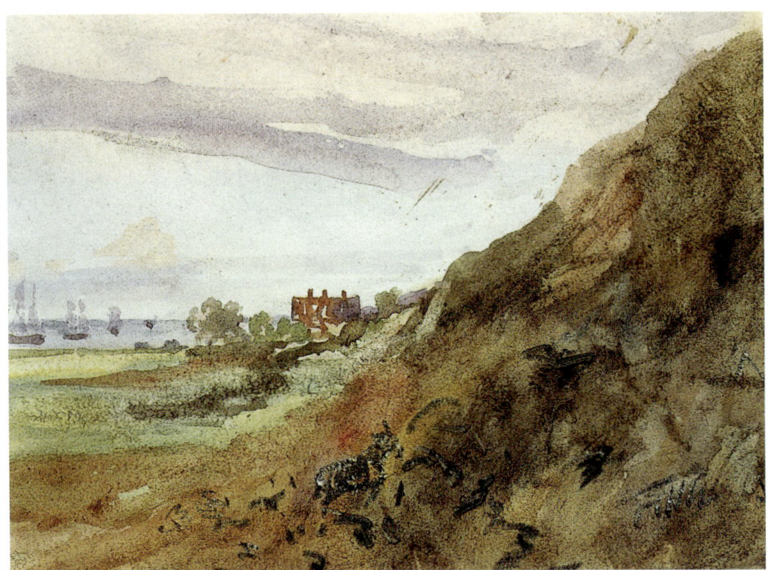

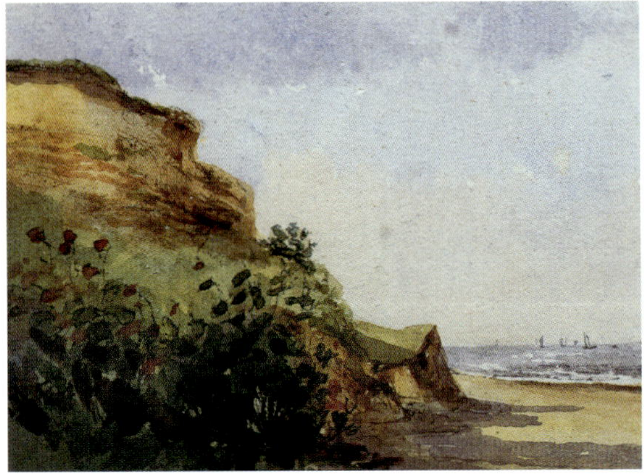

111. Felixstowe Cliffs looking North
Watercolour 3¾ x 4¾ ins
Inscribed *at Felixstowe*
Provenance: Emma
(Ref. T2)

110. The Cliffs at Felixstowe
Watercolour 5¾ x 7¾ ins
Provenance: Emma
The former Langer Lodge is seen in the distance. *(Ref. T2)*

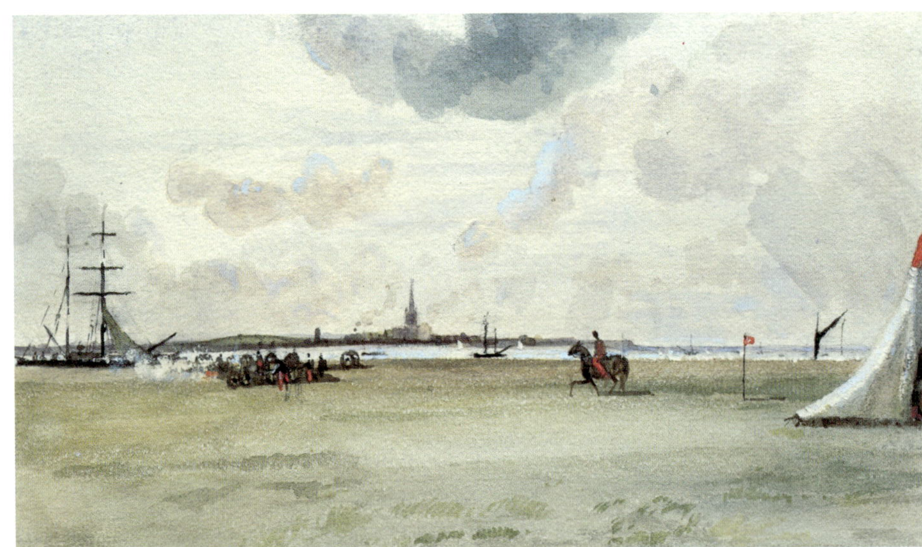

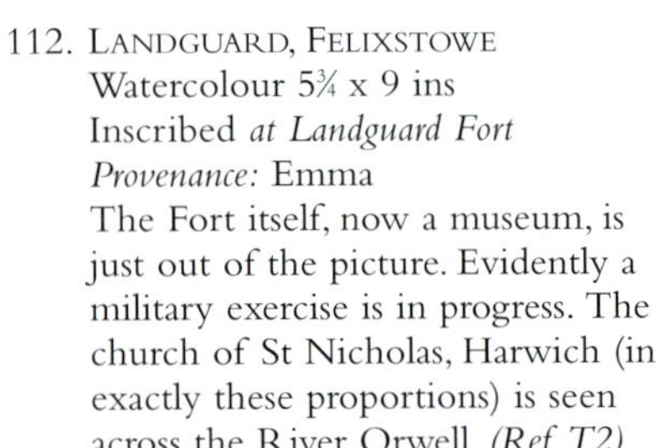

112. Landguard, Felixstowe
Watercolour 5¾ x 9 ins
Inscribed *at Landguard Fort*
Provenance: Emma
The Fort itself, now a museum, is just out of the picture. Evidently a military exercise is in progress. The church of St Nicholas, Harwich (in exactly these proportions) is seen across the River Orwell. *(Ref. T2)*

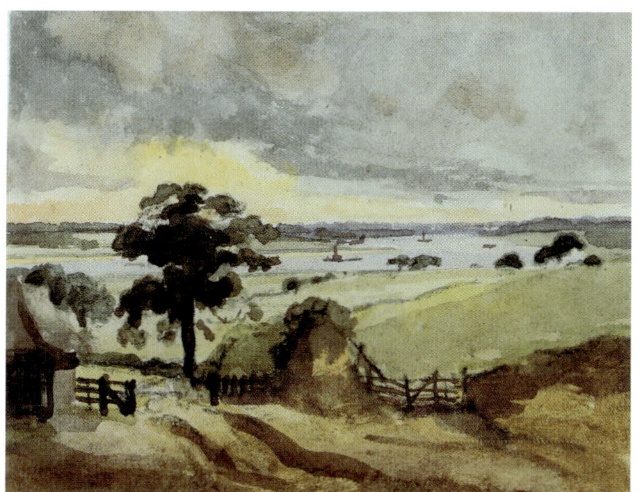

113. THE ORWELL AT TRIMLEY
Watercolour 3¾ x 4¾ ins
Inscribed *at Trimley*
Provenance: Emma
Looking towards Ipswich. *(Ref. T2)*

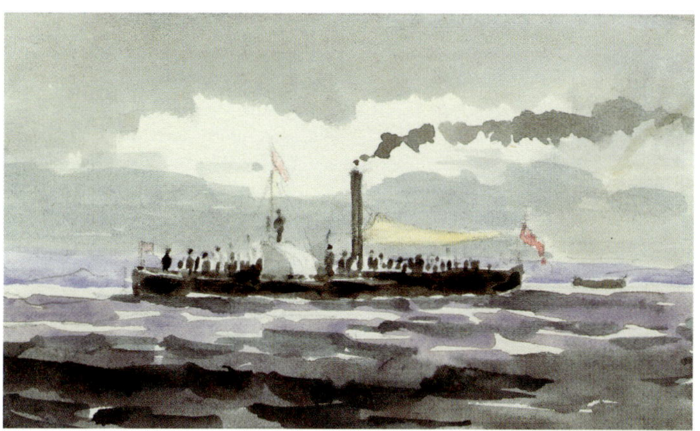

114. A PLEASURE STEAMER
Watercolour 3 x 5¼ ins
Provenance: Emma
Probably on the Orwell. *(Ref. T2)*

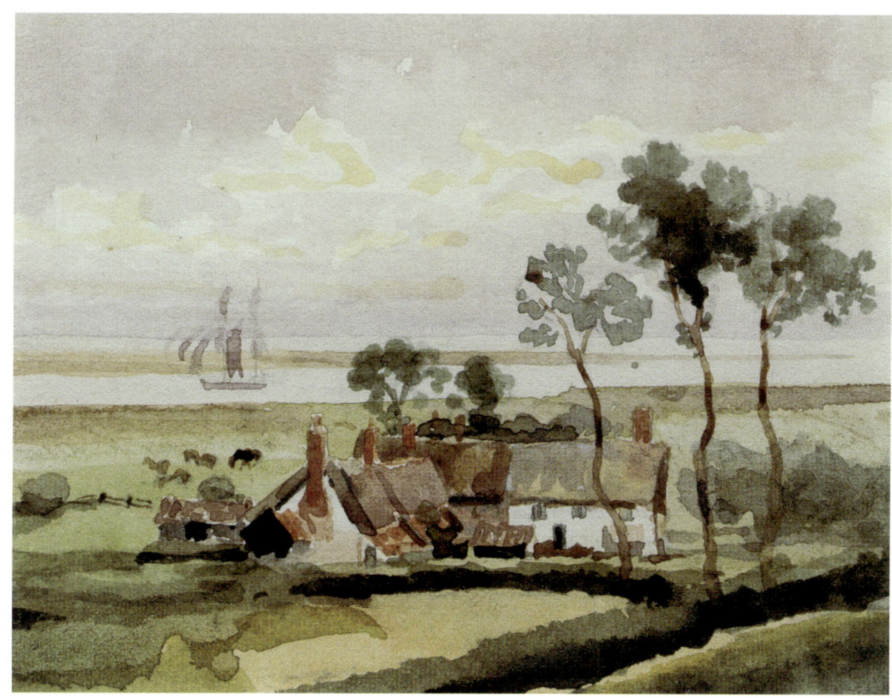

115. THE RIVER ORE AT GEDGRAVE
Watercolour 3¾ x 4¾ ins
Inscribed *Orford*
Provenance: Emma
A mile south of Orford. *(Ref. S3)*

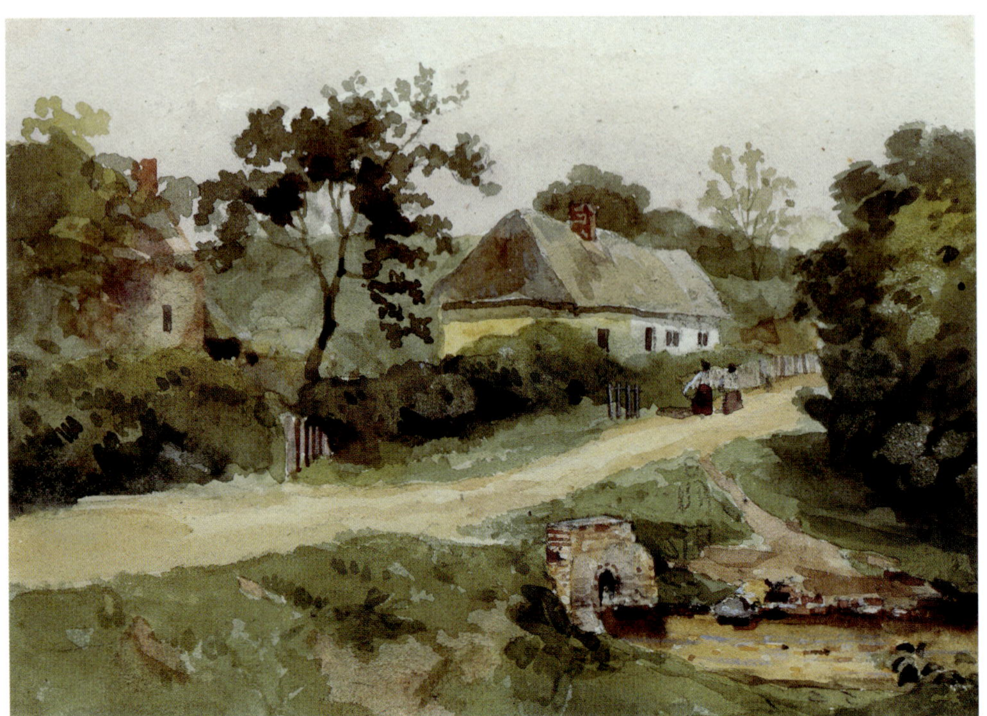

116. Butley near Orford
Watercolour 5¾ x 7¾ ins
Inscribed *at Butley*
Provenance: Emma
About 4 miles NW of Orford where the Butley River runs under the road. *(Ref. R3)*

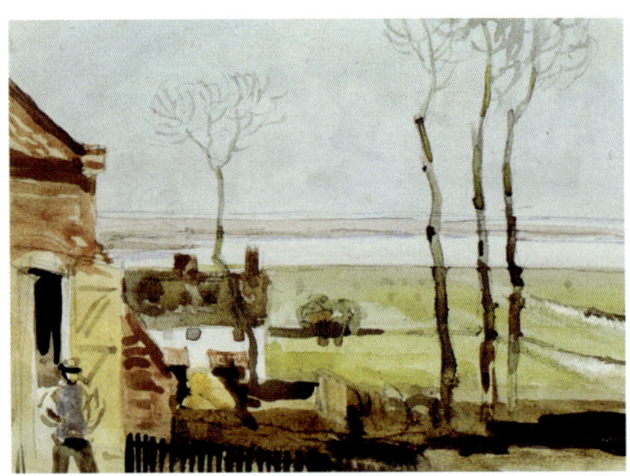

117. Gedgrave near Orford
Watercolour 3¾ x 4¾ ins
Provenance: Harriet
The same farm buildings as in 115.
(Ref. S3)

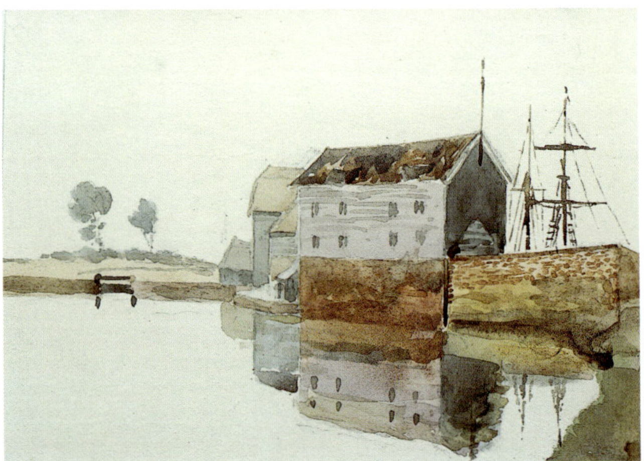

118. Boyton Dock near Orford
Watercolour 5¾ x 7¾ ins
Provenance: Harriet
On the Butley River just S.W of Gedgrave and Orford.
(Ref. S3)

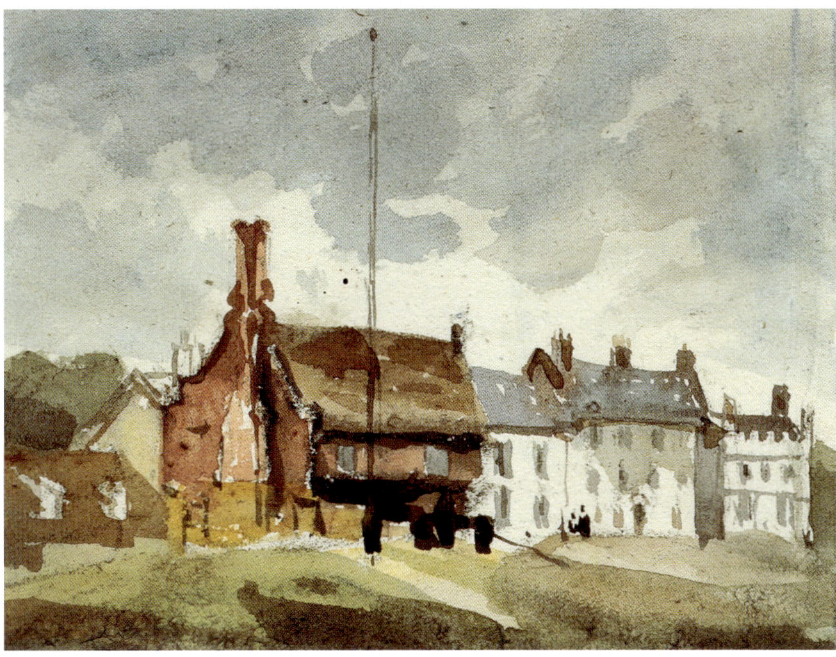

119. THE MOOT HALL, ALDEBURGH
Watercolour 3¾ x 4¾ ins
Provenance: Emma
The tall Tudor-style chimney was only built in 1854, showing this to be a comparatively late work. Aldeburgh, 'that delightful bathing place', was the Churchyard family's most favoured holiday resort. TC's daughters continued their visits after he died. *(Ref. R4)*

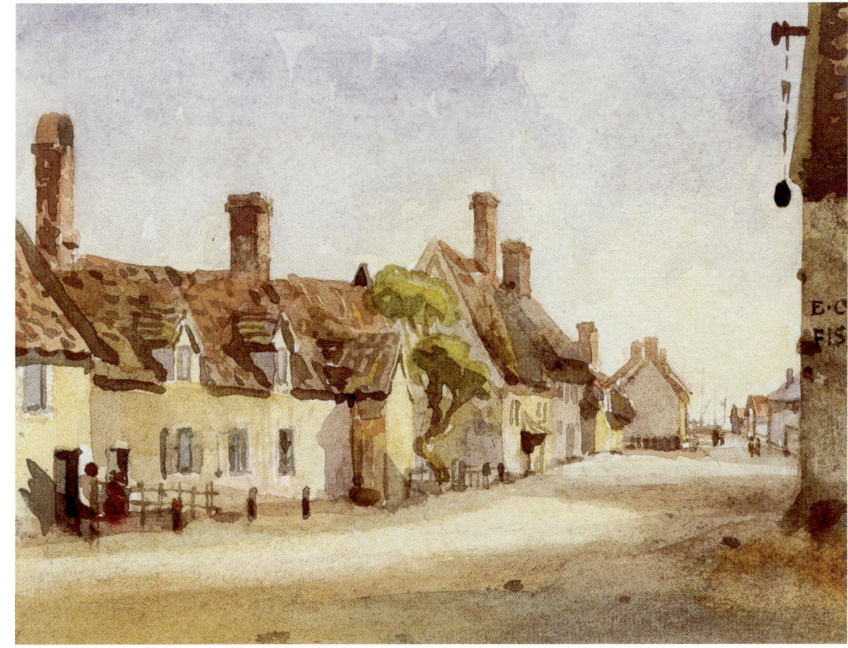

120. HIGH STREET, ALDEBURGH
Watercolour 3¾ x 4¾ ins
Inscribed *at Aldbro*
Provenance: Emma
Edward Coe, the fish-merchant whose name figures on the building to the right, is recorded in Aldeburgh in 1855 but not in 1844. This view of the High Street looks south towards the quay at Slaughden. *(Ref. R4)*

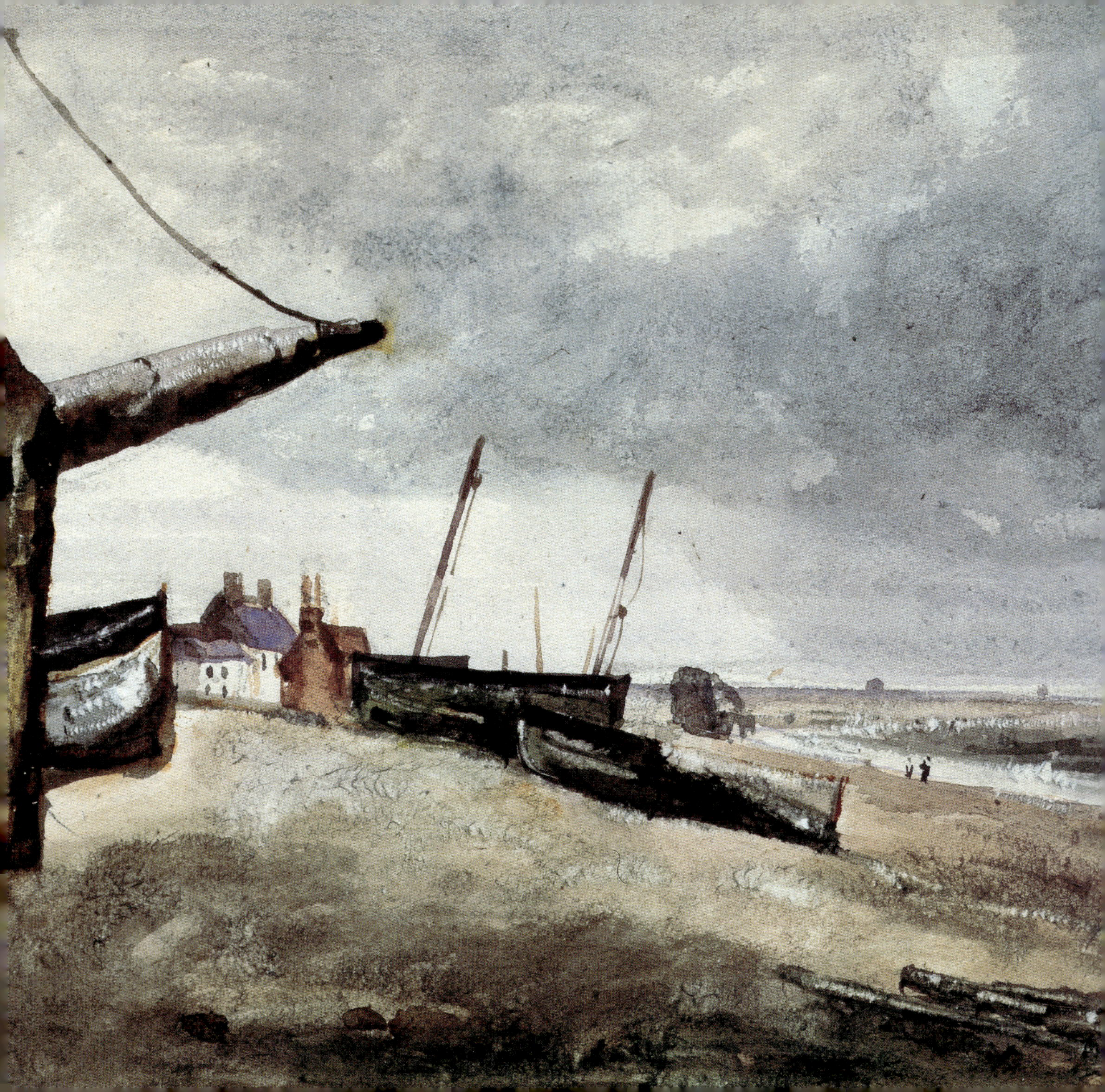

121. Aldeburgh Beach looking North
Watercolour 6 x 7¾ ins
Inscribed *at Albro*
Provenance: Emma
Post 1854. What is now Thorpeness is seen on the horizon. *(Ref. R4)*

122. Summer, Aldeburgh
Black chalk on toned paper 5 x 6 ins
Provenance: Emma
Probably Churchyard's wife, one of his elder daughters and his youngest son Charles (Charley, born 1841) comprise the nearest group. *(Ref. R4)*

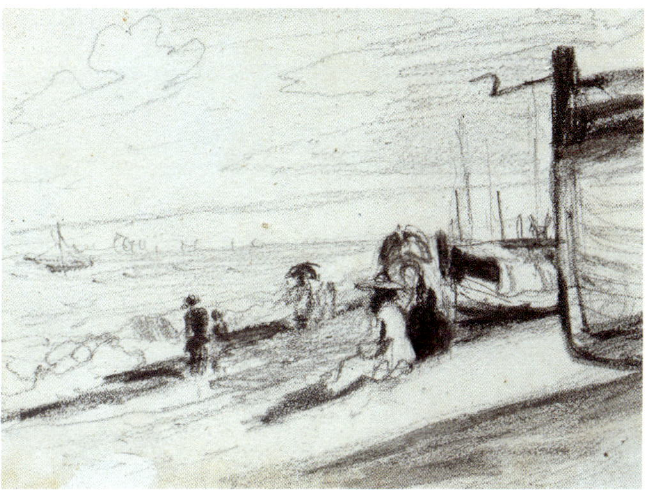

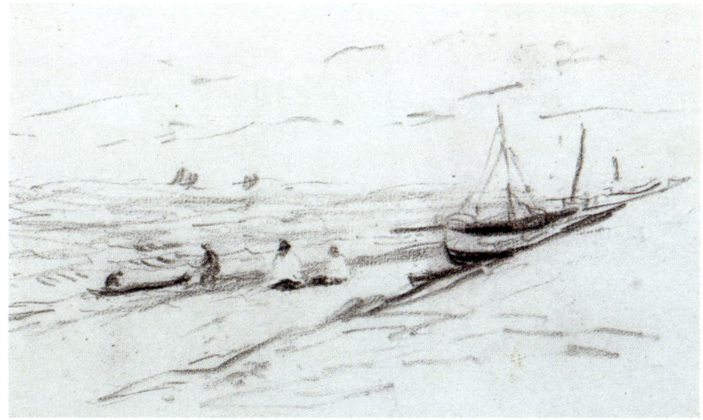

123. Sketch of Aldeburgh Seafront
Black chalk 3½ x 6 ins *(Ref. R4)*
Provenance: Emma

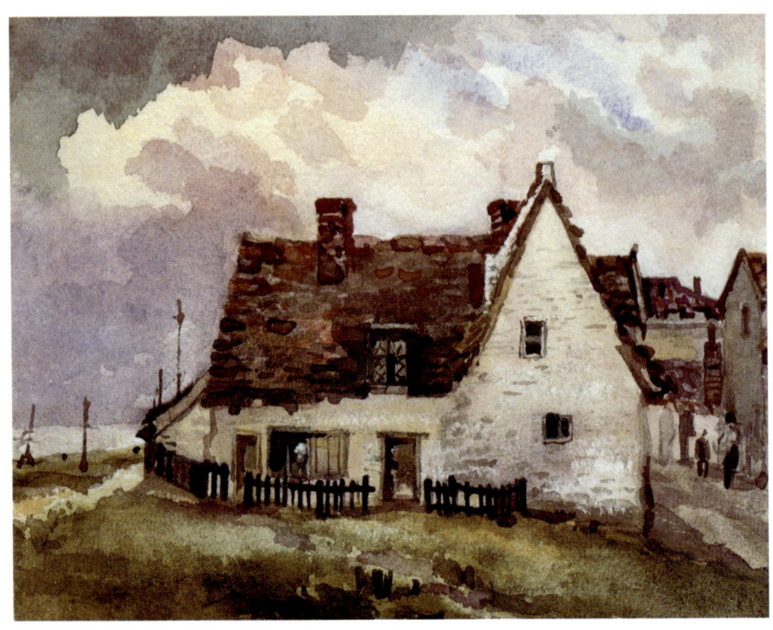

124. Fisherman's Cottage, Aldeburgh
Watercolour 3¾ x 4¾ ins *(Ref. R4)*
Provenance: Harriet

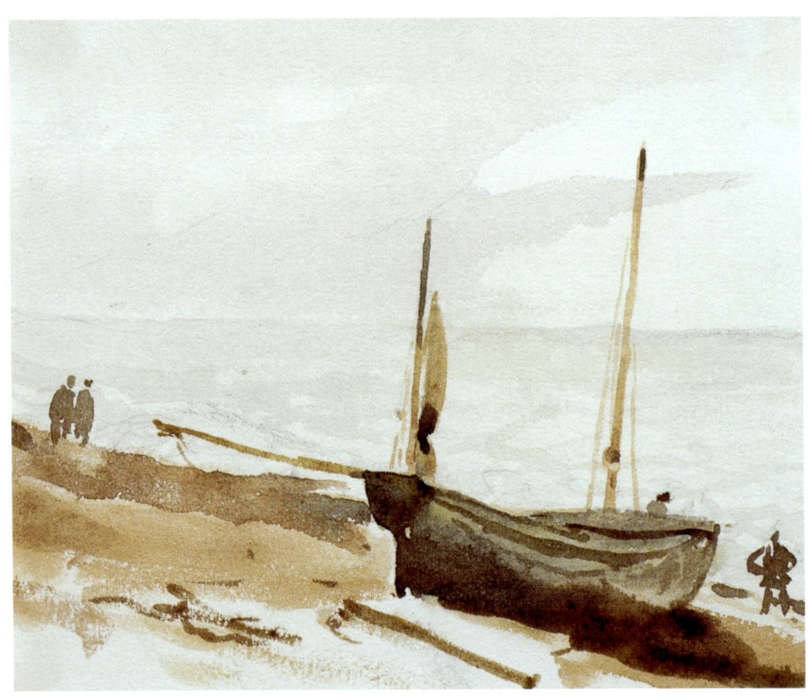

125. Beached Boat, Aldeburgh
Watercolour 4¼ x 5 ins *(Ref. R4)*
Provenance: Harriet

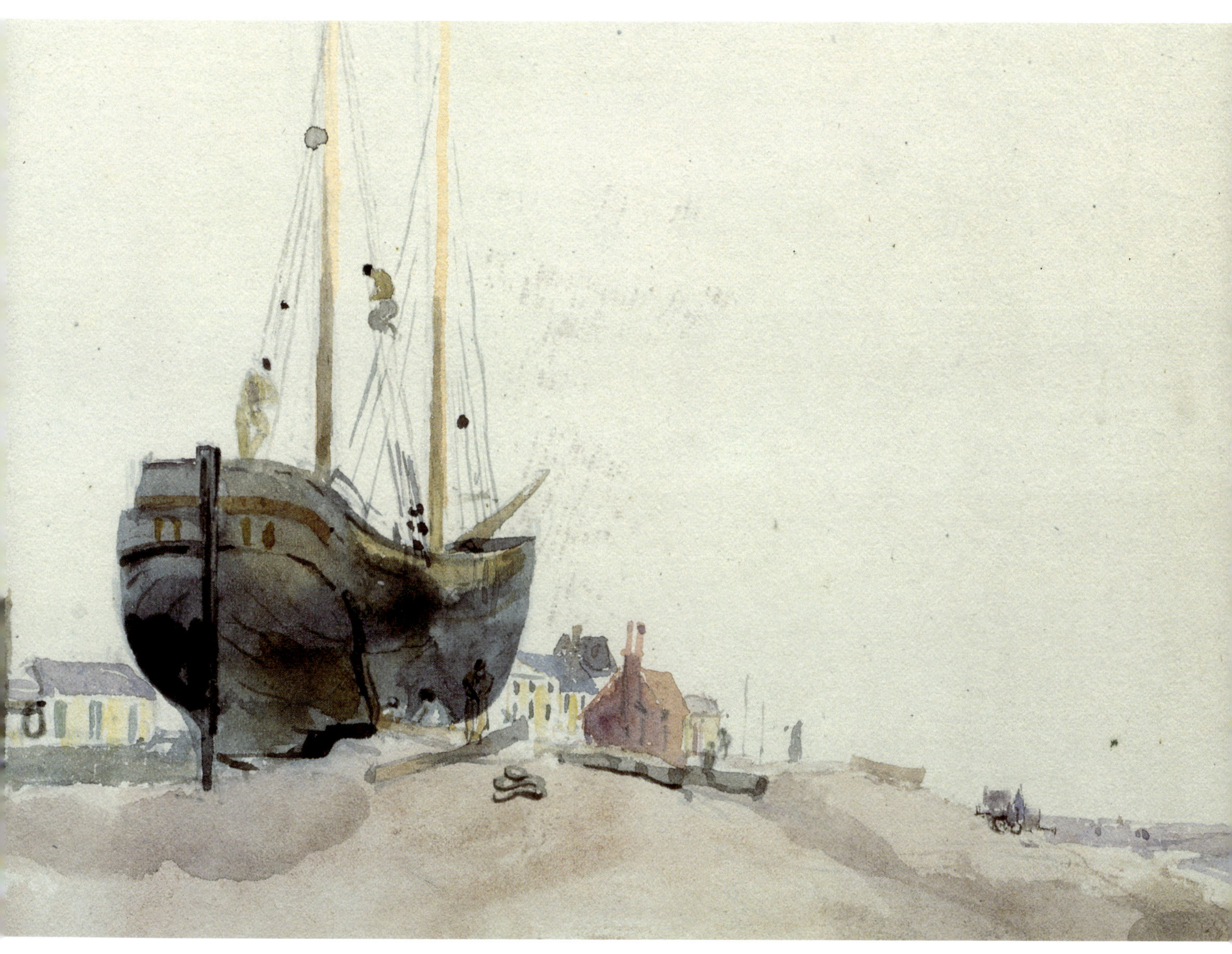

126. Schooner Ashore, Aldeburgh
Watercolour 5¾ x 7¾ ins
Provenance: Harriet
Post 1854. So large a boat can only rarely have been pulled up the pebble beach. *(Ref. R4)*

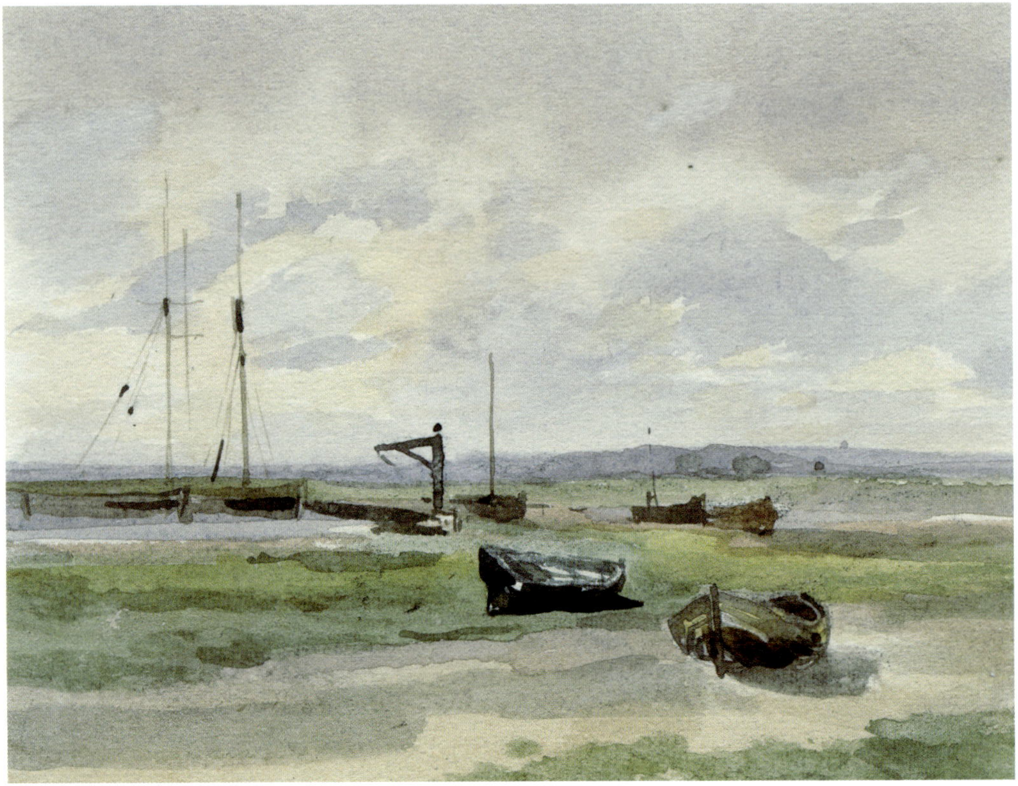

127. Fishing Boats, River Beyond
Watercolour 3¾ x 4¾ ins
Provenance: Harriet
Possibly by the River Alde near Slaughden, a mile south of Aldeburgh.
(Ref. R4)

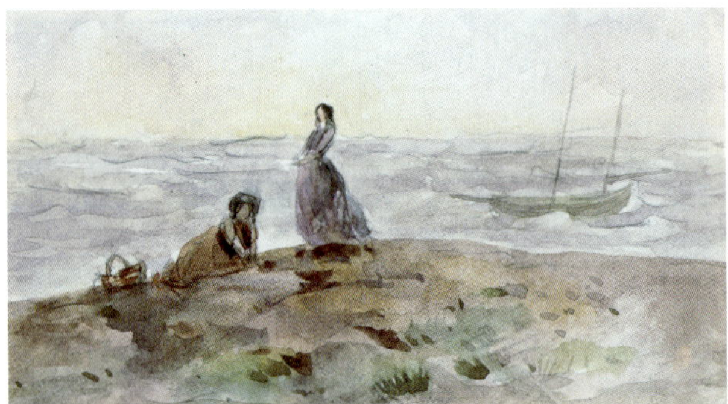

128. Gathering Flowers on the Foreshore
Watercolour 2½ x 4¼ ins
Provenance: Emma
Resembles the shingle foreshore at Aldeburgh. *(Ref. R4)*
Verso: Tree Study with House
Pencil

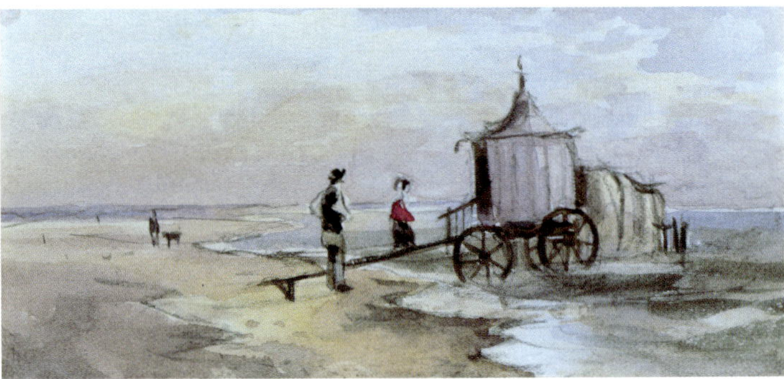

129. A Bathing-Machine, Suffolk Coast
Watercolour 2½ x 5 ins
Provenance: Harriet
Probably Aldeburgh or Southwold. *(Ref. R4)*
Verso: Detail from a Legal Document

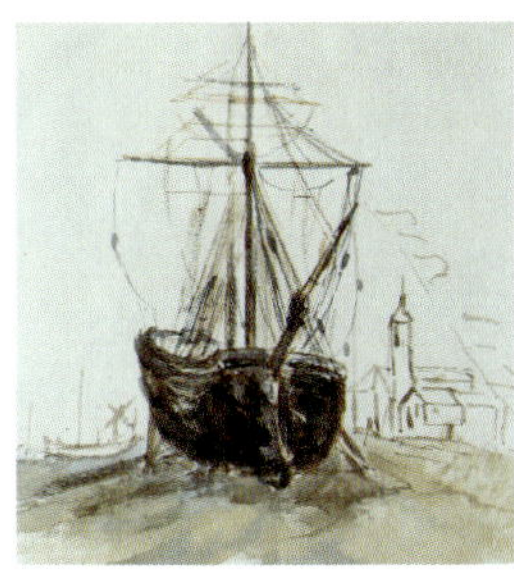

130. Schooner in Stocks, Aldeburgh
Pen and ink and sepia wash 7¼ x 6½ ins
Provenance: Harriet
A coastguard lookout and a windmill are seen in the distance. *(Ref. R4)*
Verso: Sketch of Mannel and Harbour Scene

131. Beached Boats
Watercolour 5¾ x 7¾ ins
Provenance: Emma
This and the next nine entries have not been located. Churchyard not only spent holidays on the coast with his daughters but often made brief visits at other times. For instance, it is recorded that in the 1850s Churchyard accompanied Thomas Carlyle on a visit to Hollesley Bay *(Ref. S3)* where he devoted himself to painting while the latter went for a sail. *(Ref. S3)*

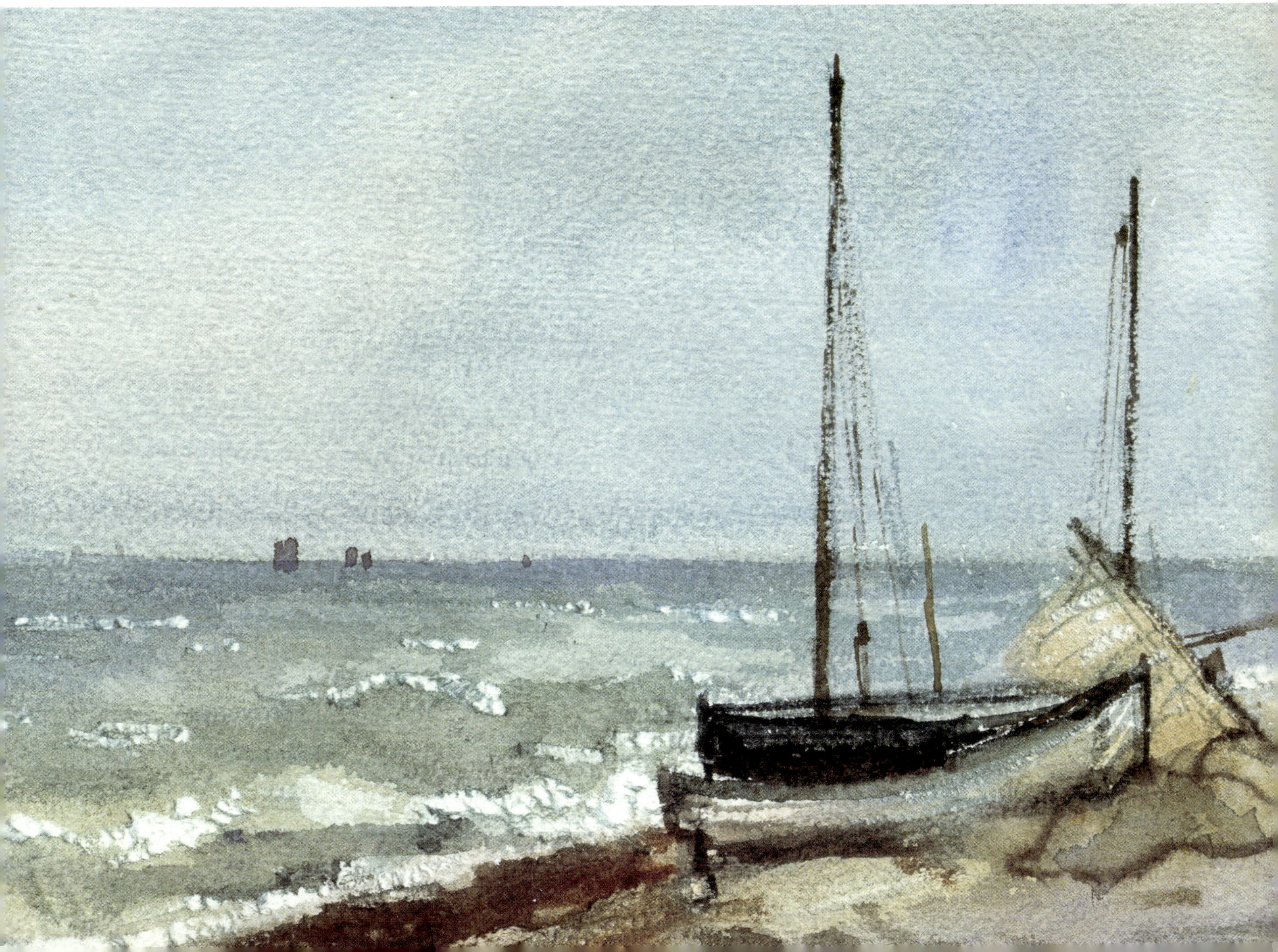

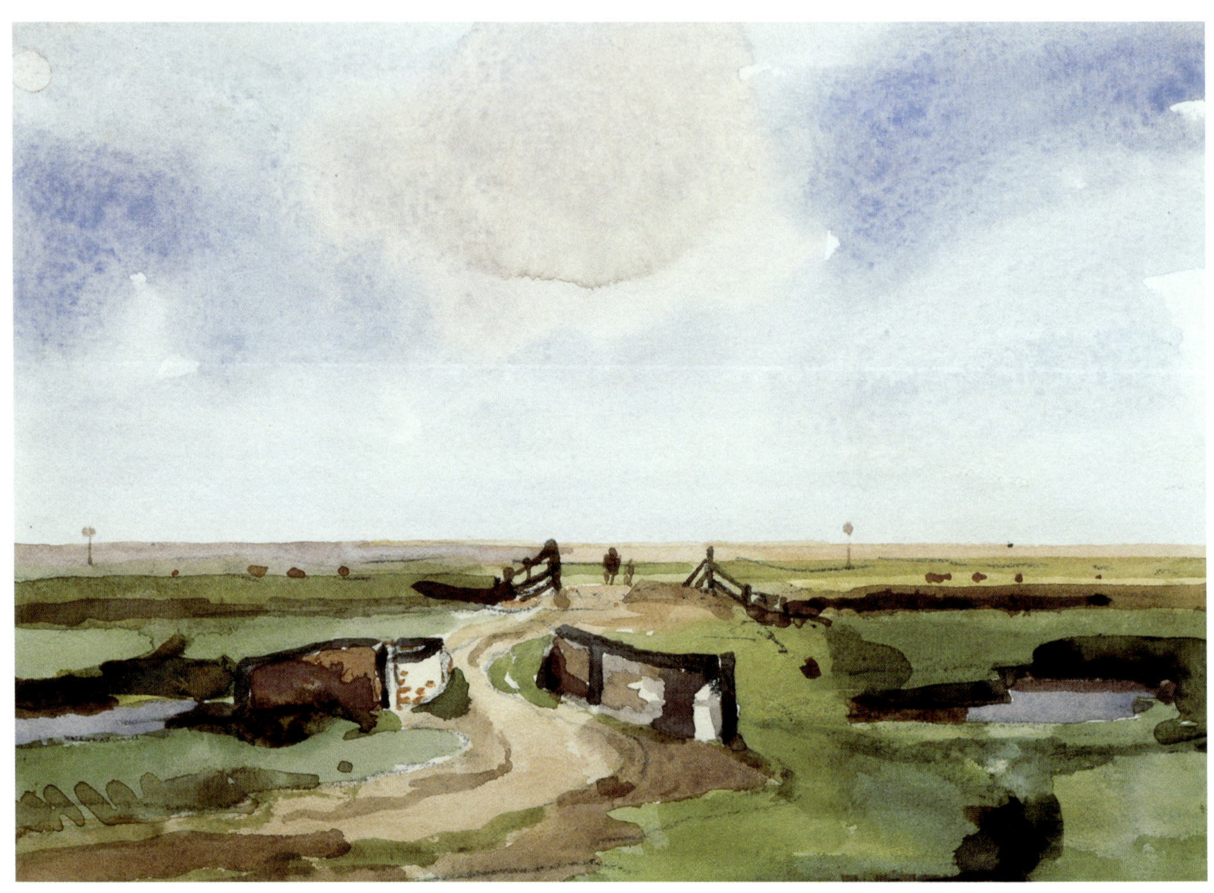

132. Marsh Road intersected by Water
Watercolour 5¾ x 7¾ ins
Provenance: Harriet

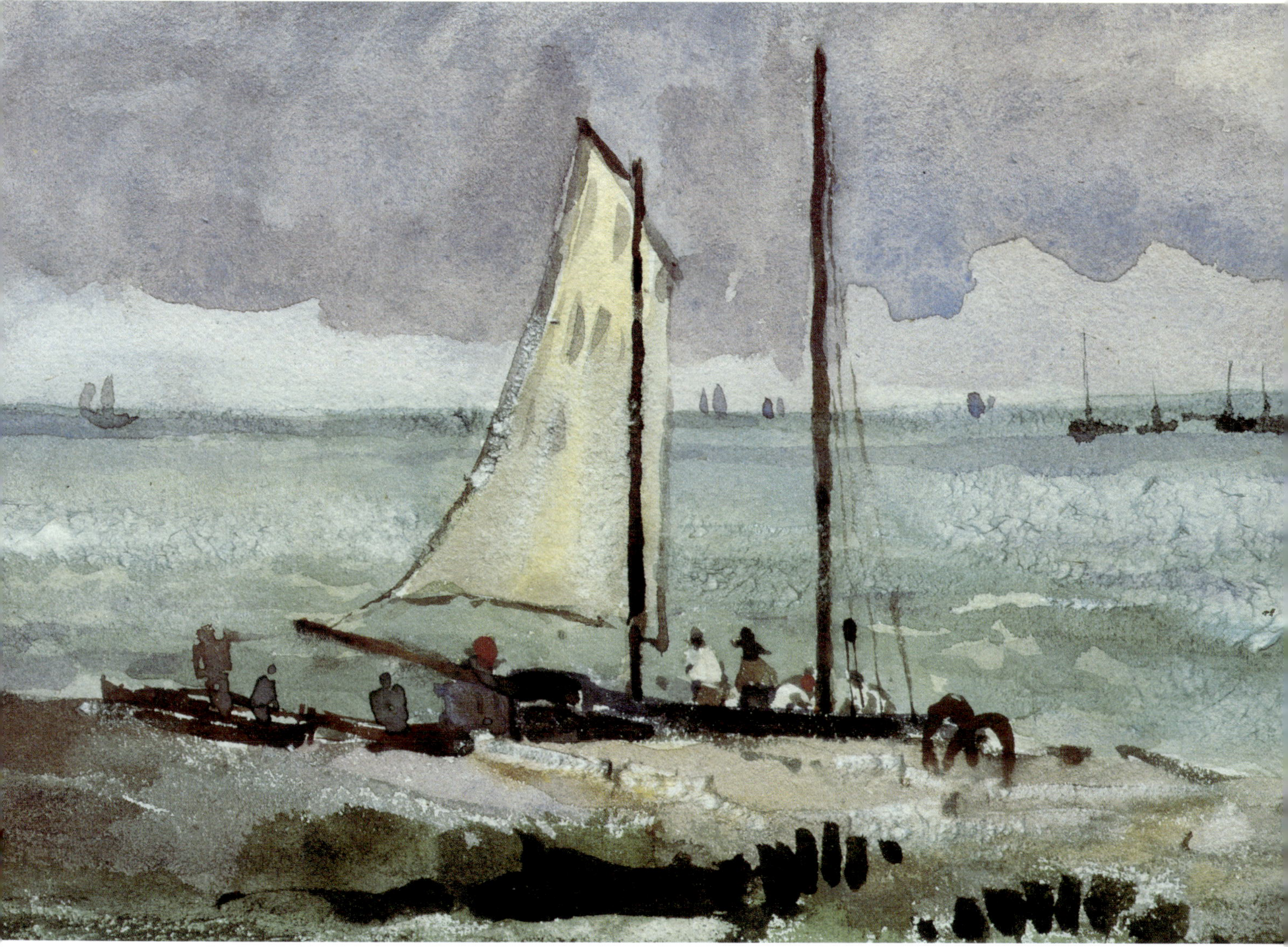

133. Boats Sheltering, Green Sea
Watercolour 4 x 6 ins
Provenance: Harriet

134. Lone Figure, Sunrise *(see back cover)*
Watercolour 5 x 7¾ ins
Provenance: Harriet
This unusual picture could in part be imaginary, as indeed are many of Churchyard's works. Note how he has captured the curviture of the distant horizon, which is both scientifically and aesthetically satisfying.

135. ROUGH SEAS, SUFFOLK COAST
Pen and ink on blue paper 4¾ x 8 ins
Provenance: Harriet

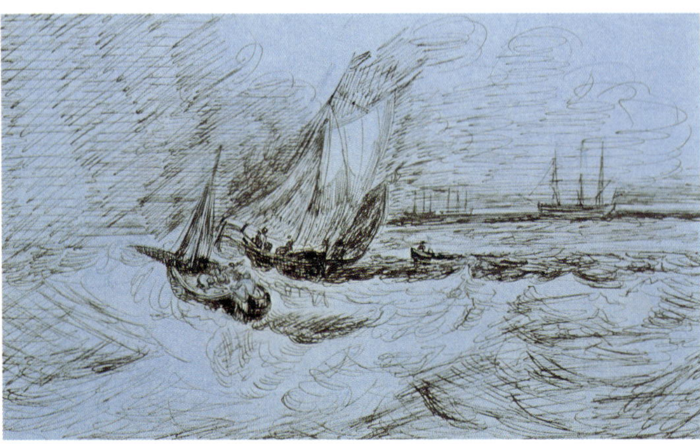

137. THE VILLAGE SQUARE
Sepia wash 4¾ x 7 ins
Provenance: Harriet
Possibly the chimney of Aldeburgh Moot Hall in the distance.

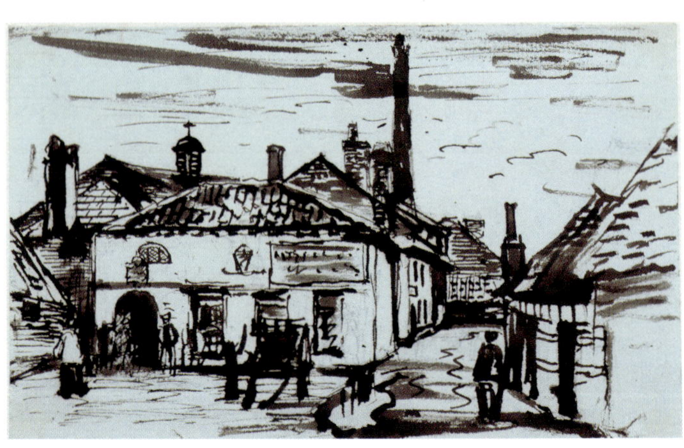

136. STREET SCENE
Pen and ink on blue paper 4¾ x 5 ins
Provenance: Harriet
Lowestoft a possibility.

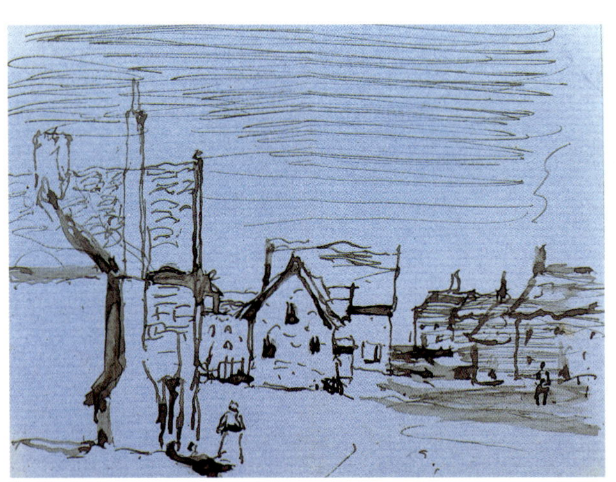

138. A CONSULTATION ON THE SHORE
Black chalk 2¾ x 5½ ins
Provenance: Harriet
Churchyard here recalls a favourite theme of Aelbert Cuyp.

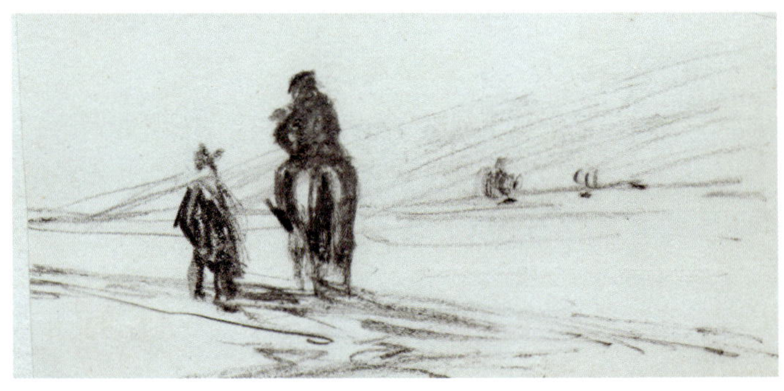

139. A Fisherman at Home
Pencil 5½ x 3¼ ins
Provenance: Harriet
A study in contrasted mood!
Verso: Fisherman with Cart

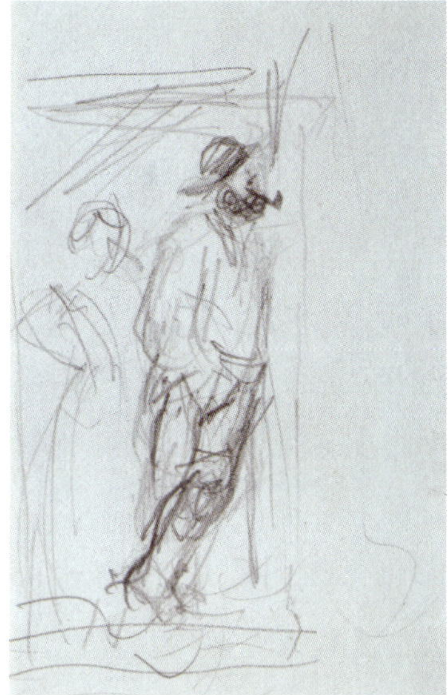

141. The Cliffs at Dunwich
Watercolour 3¾ x 4¾ ins
Provenance: Harriet
Cliffs which have suffered constant coast erosion. *(Ref. P4)*

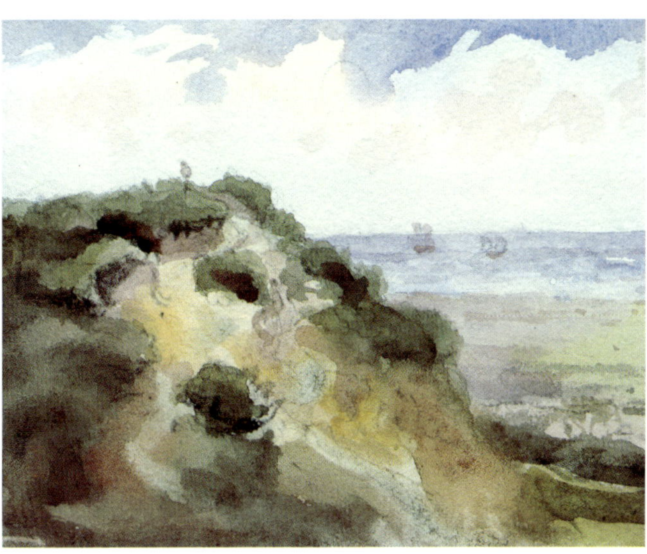

140. A Fleet of Yachts
Black chalk on buff paper 3½ x 5 ins
Provenance: Harriet
Creating highlights by scuffing the paper was a device Churchyard constantly employed, though rarely as extensively as in this picture.

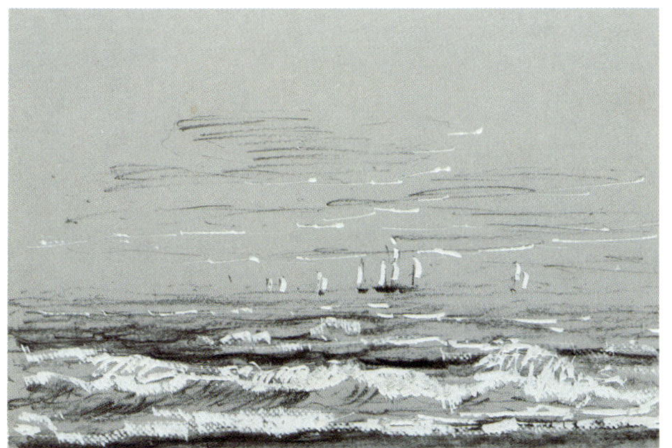

142. The Signpost at Yoxford
Pen and ink 3¼ x 5½ ins
Provenance: Harriet
A famous metal signpost which still stands in Yoxford churchyard. It points to London 93 miles, Framlingham 10 miles and Yarmouth 30 miles. *(Ref. Q3)*

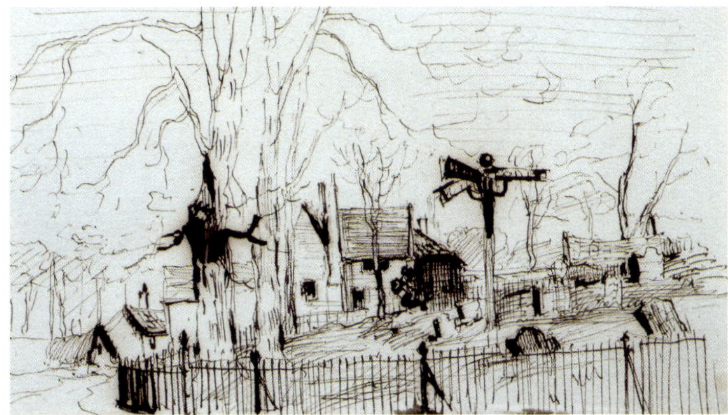

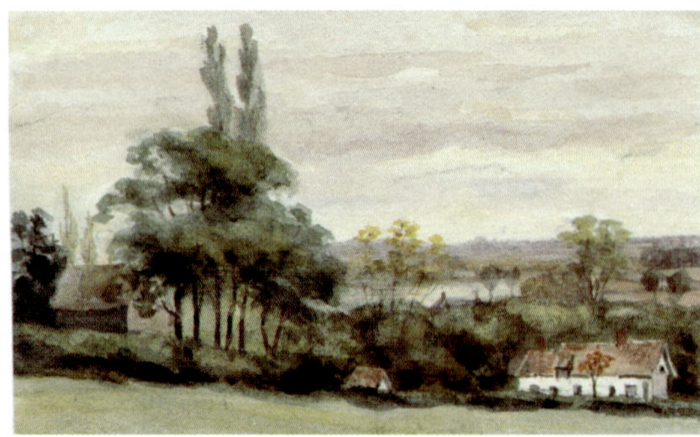

143. NEAR HALESWORTH
Watercolour 3 x 5 ins
Inscribed *at Halesworth*
Provenance: Emma
Some 10 miles inland from Southwold. It was in Halesworth, many years before, that Churchyard was articled as a solicitor. *(Ref. P3)*

144. THE BEACH AT SOLE BAY
Watercolour 5¼ x 8¾ ins
Provenance: Harriet
From Dunwich looking north towards Walberswick and Southwold. *(Ref. P4)*

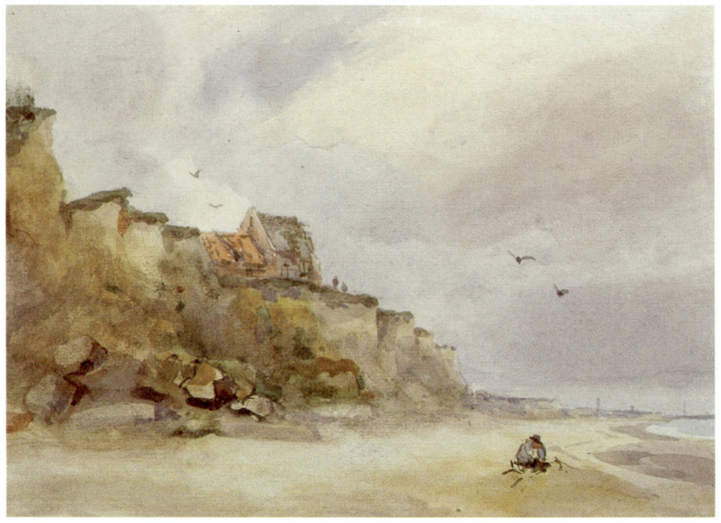

145. COTTAGES AT COVEHITHE
Watercolour 5¾ x 8 ins
Provenance: Harriet
Sadly these cottages have long since disappeared as a result of coast erosion. *(Ref. O5)*

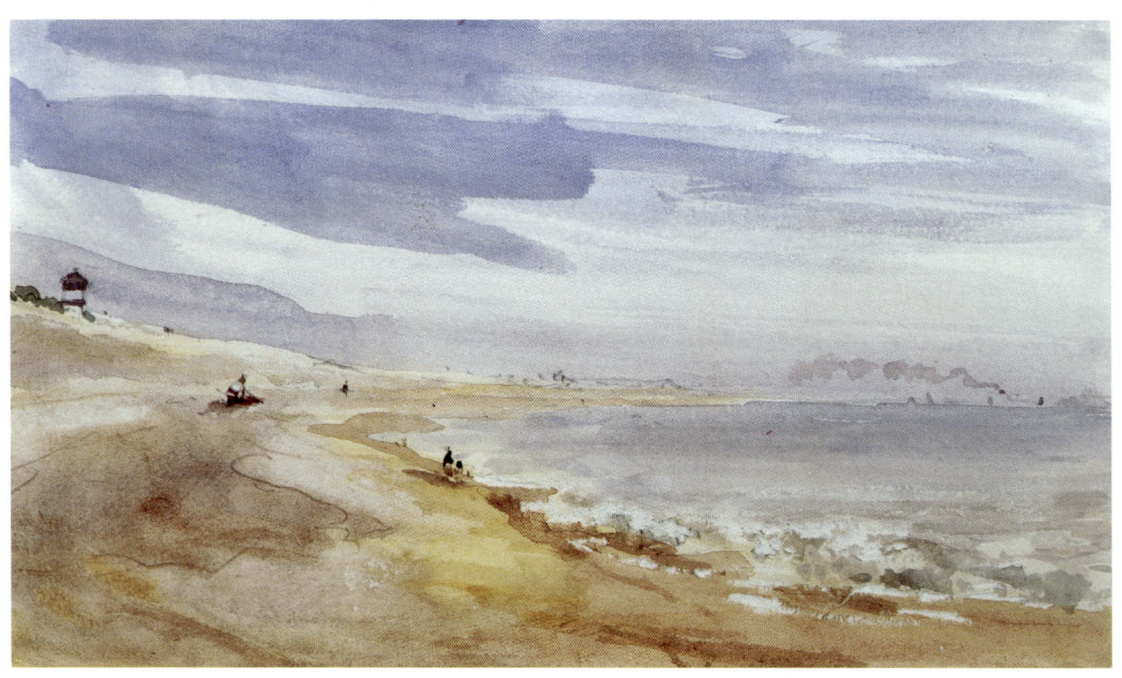

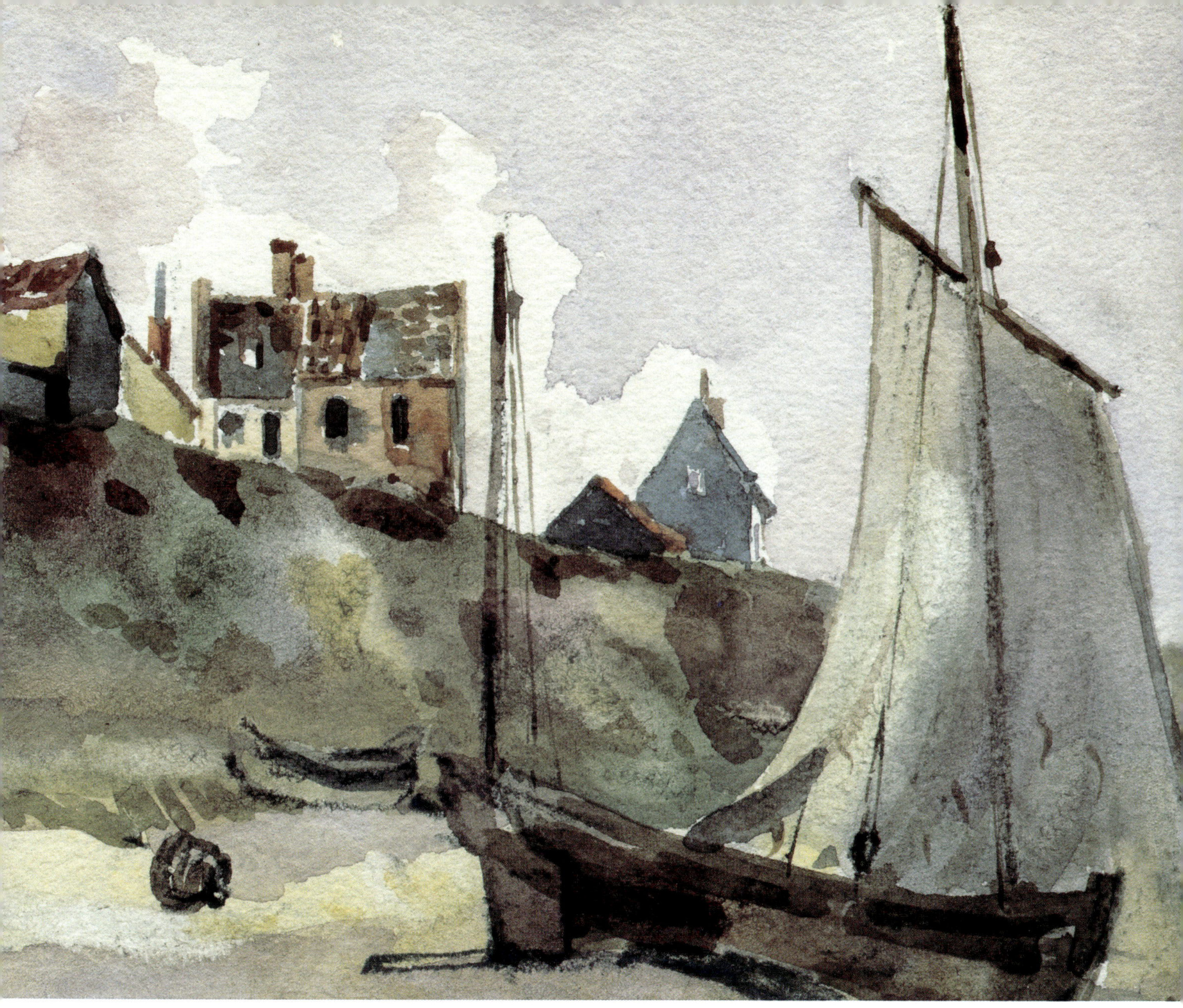

146. Cottages at Pakefield
Watercolour 3¾ x 4¾ ins
Provenance: Harriet
These too were lost as the coast receded. The Churchyards appear more than once to have stayed in or near Lowestoft judging by the number of paintings of the neighbourhood both father and daughters produced. *(Ref. N5)*

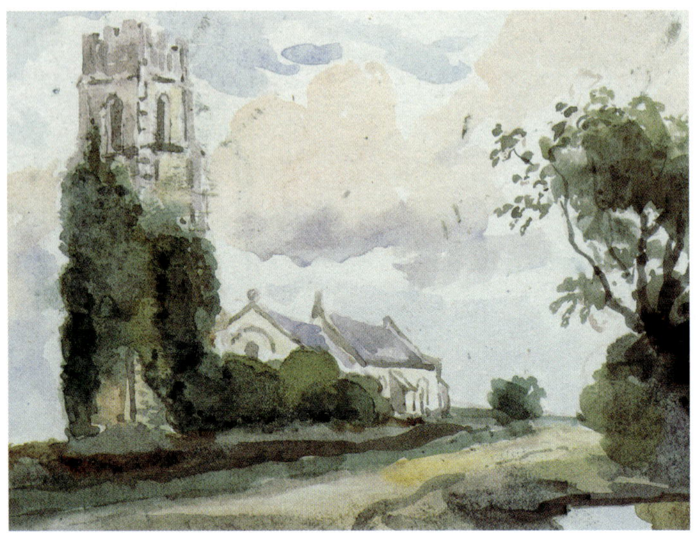

147. Corton Church near Lowestoft
Watercolour 4½ x 6 ins
Provenance: Emma
The tower still stands though without the ivy cladding. *(Ref. N5)*

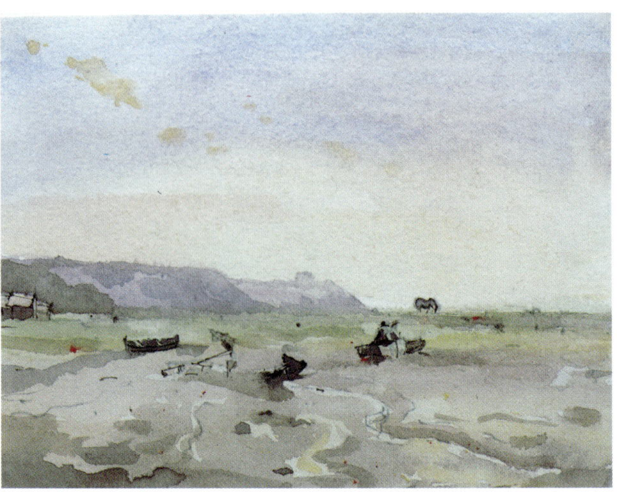

149. Extensive Sandy Beach
Watercolour 3¾ x 4¾ ins
Provenance: Emma
Probably in the Lowestoft neighbourhood.

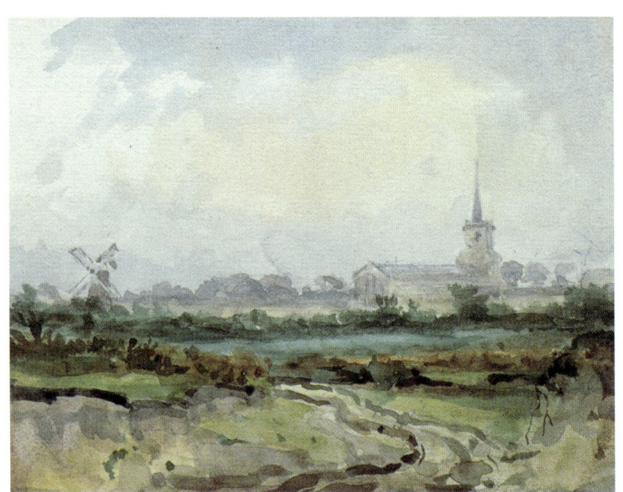

148. St Margaret's Church, Lowestoft
Watercolour 3¾ x 4¾ ins *(Ref. N5)*
Provenance: Emma

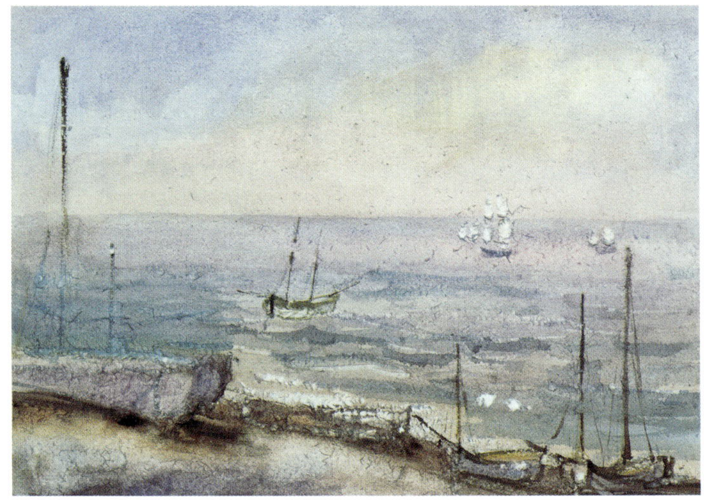

150. Shipping off Lowestoft
Watercolour 5¾ x 7¾ ins
Provenance: Emma
With the customary scratching out.

151. Three Sailing Boats
Pencil 3¾ x 5¾ ins
Provenance: Emma

152. Church Tower, Beccles
Pencil 5½ x 3¼ ins *(Ref. N4)*
Provenance: Harriet

153. Quayside, Lowestoft
Watercolour 3½ x 7 ins *(Ref. N5)*
Provenance: Harriet

154. Drainage Mills near Yarmouth
Pencil 2¼ x 8 ins *(Ref. M4)*
Provenance: Emma

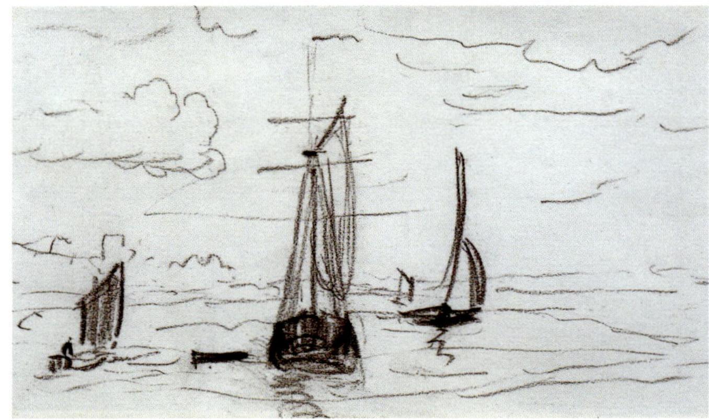

151.

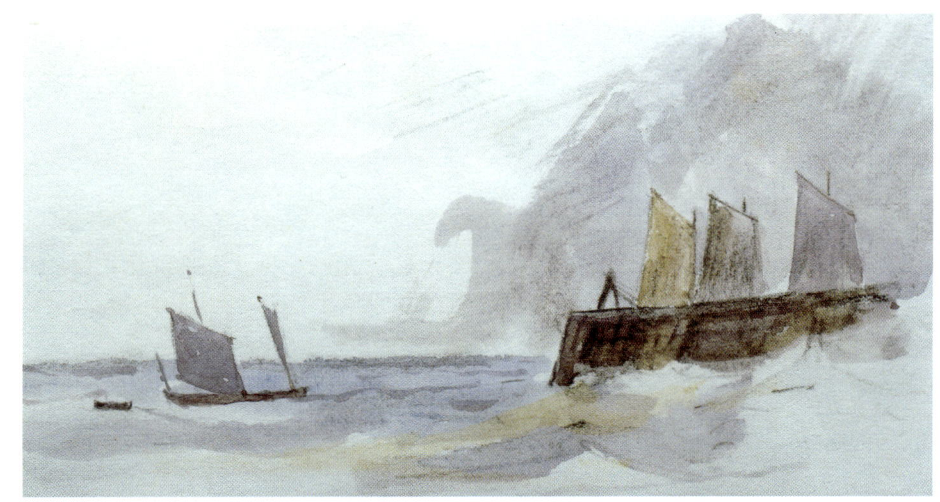

153.

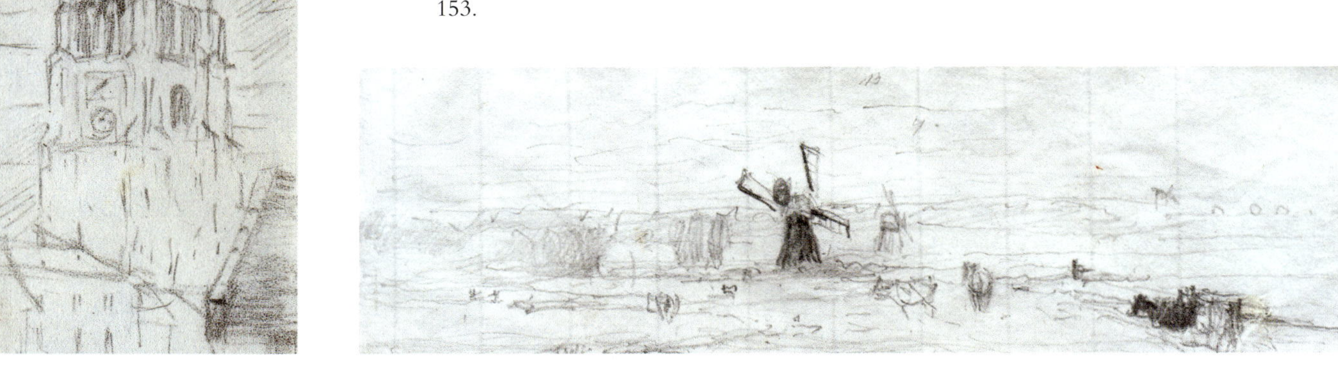

152.

154.

Elsewhere in England

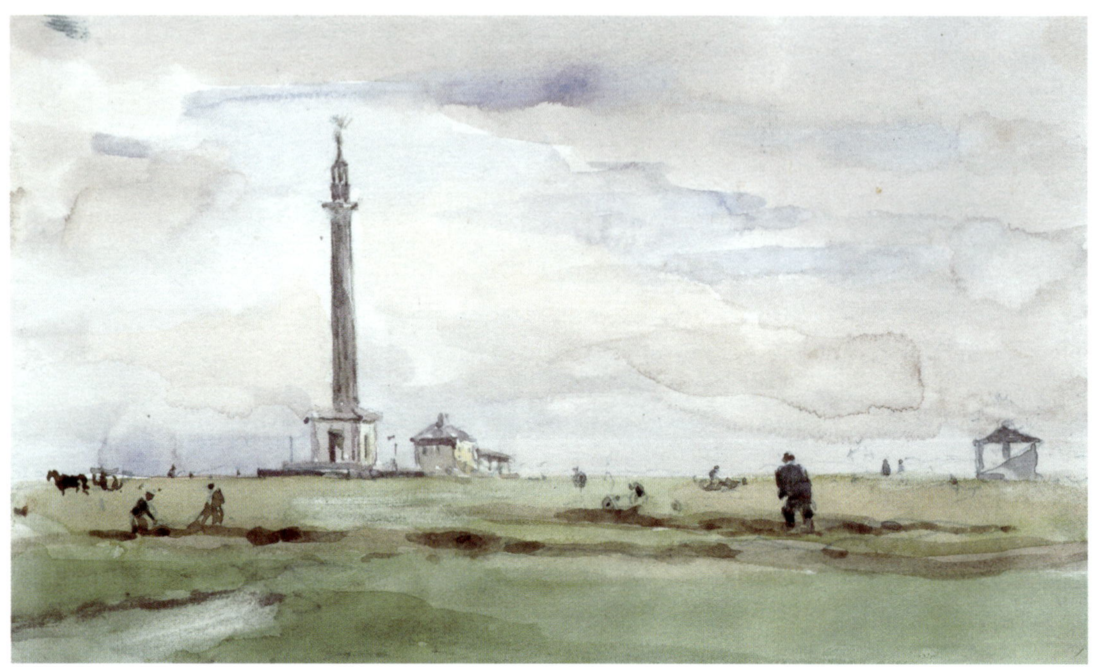

155. Nelson's Column, Yarmouth
Watercolour 4½ x 7 ins
Provenance: Emma
Designed by William Wilkins, architect of the National Gallery in Trafalgar Square, and erected in 1819. The figure is not Nelson but Britannia who faces inland towards Nelson's birthplace. *(Ref. M5)*

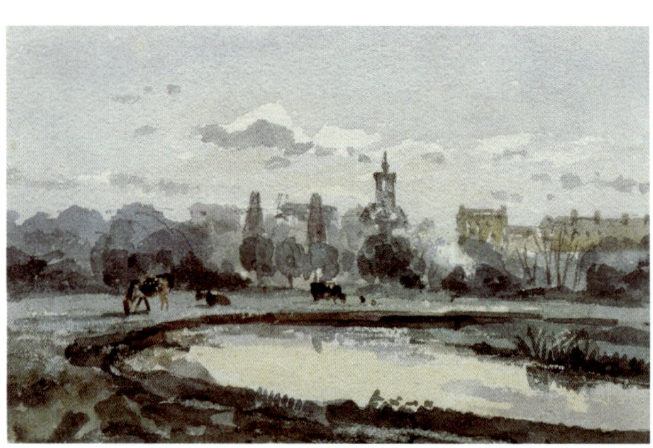

156. Stamford Hill, Tottenham
Watercolour 4½ x 6 ins
Inscribed *Stamford Hill*
Provenance: Emma
Churchyard was a regular visitor to London, in later life more often as a collector than as a lawyer.

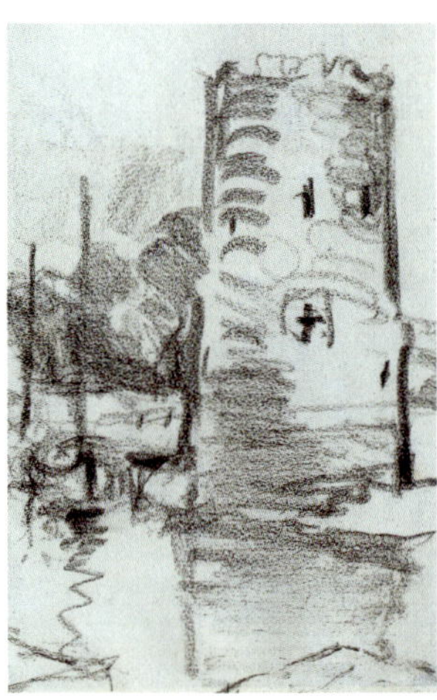

157. The Cow Tower, Norwich
Black chalk 5½ x 3¼ ins
Provenance: Emma
A much-favoured subject of the Norwich School of painters.

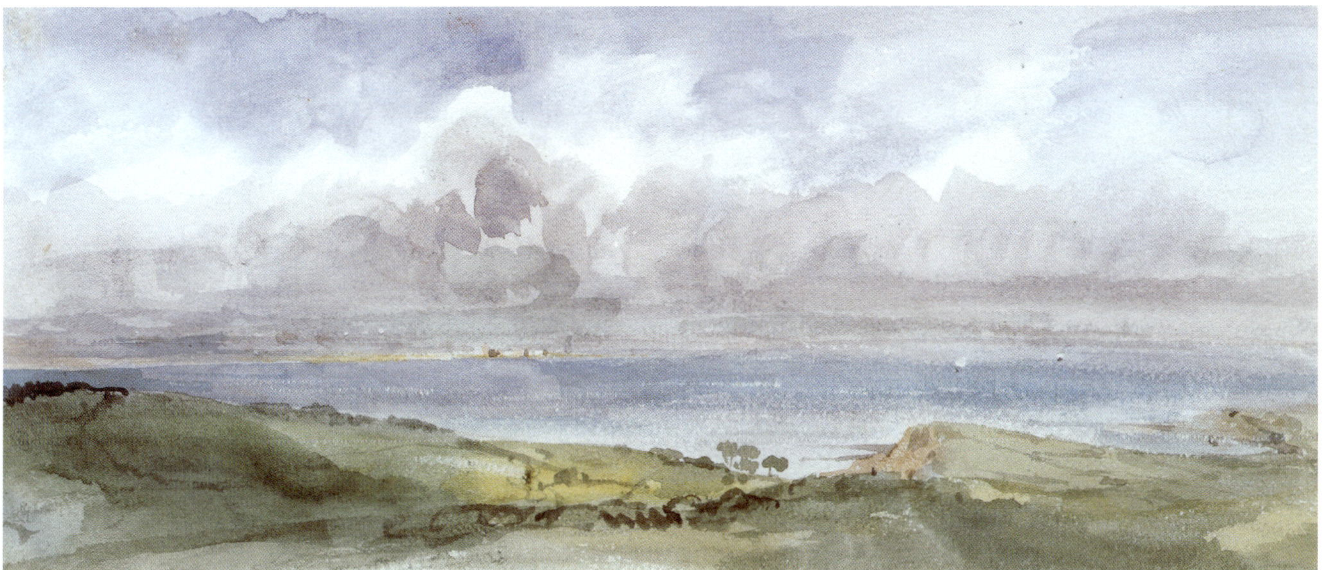

158. The Isle of Wight
Watercolour 4½ x 10½ ins
Inscribed *In the Isle of Wight*
Provenance: Emma
This is the sole specific evidence of a visit to the island, although Churchyard appears to have taken his daughters on occasional trips to the south coast, as well as at least one trip to Weston-super-Mare on the Bristol Channel. Once or twice he also travelled to the south-west in his youth. This painting is clearly a late work, however, as are virtually all the watercolours in this collection.

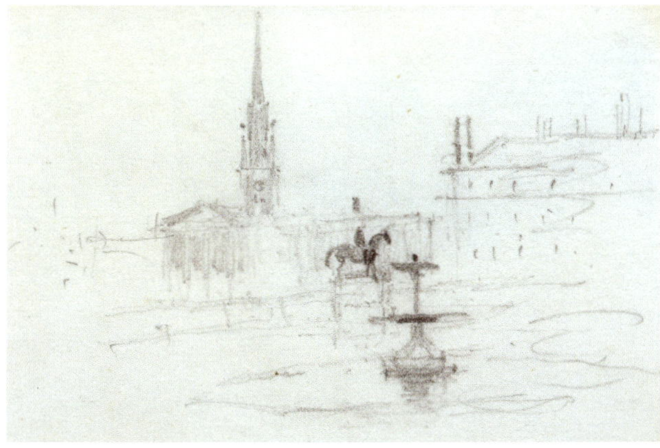

159. Trafalgar Square, London
Pencil 3¼ x 5¼ ins
Provenance: Emma
With centre the church of St Martin-in-the-Fields.

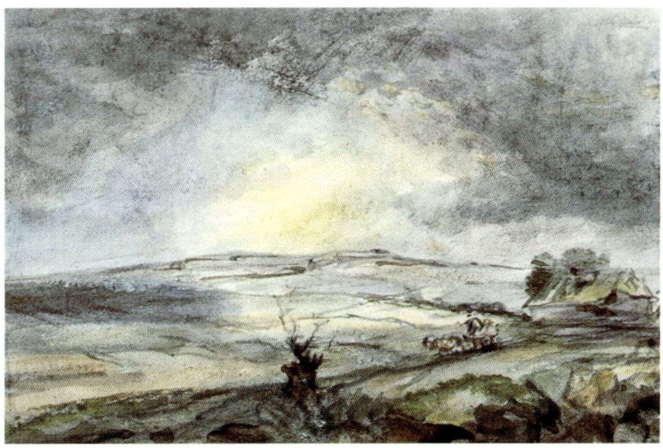

160. Sombre Scene with Horse-drawn Carriage
Watercolour 5¼ x 8 ins
Provenance: Emma
An unusually dramatised composition which offers little clue as to its location. Probably a figment of his imagination.

Location Map for Drawings in the Woodbridge and Deben Areas c. 1835

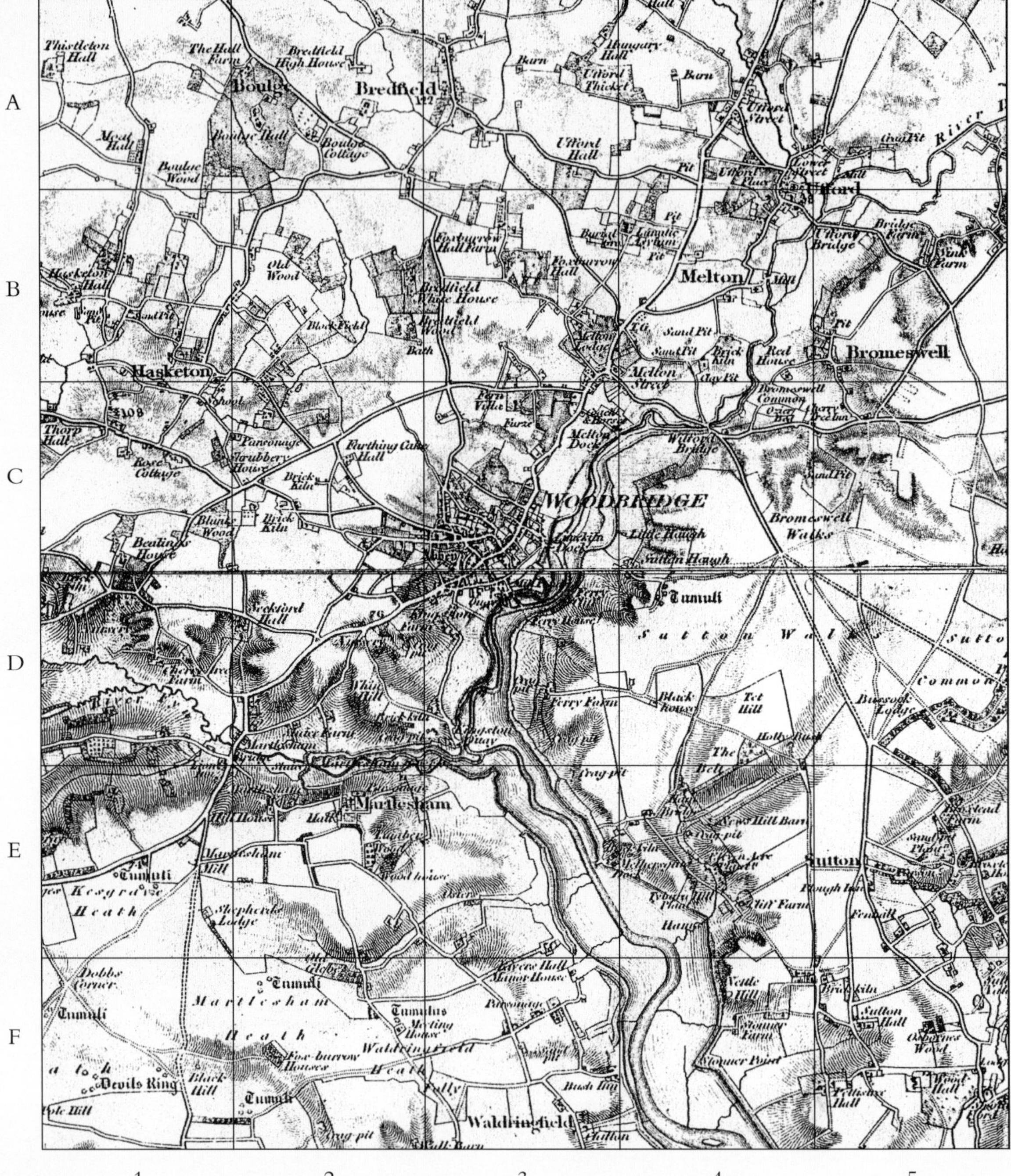

Location Map
for Drawings
in the Suffolk
Coastal Area
c. 1840

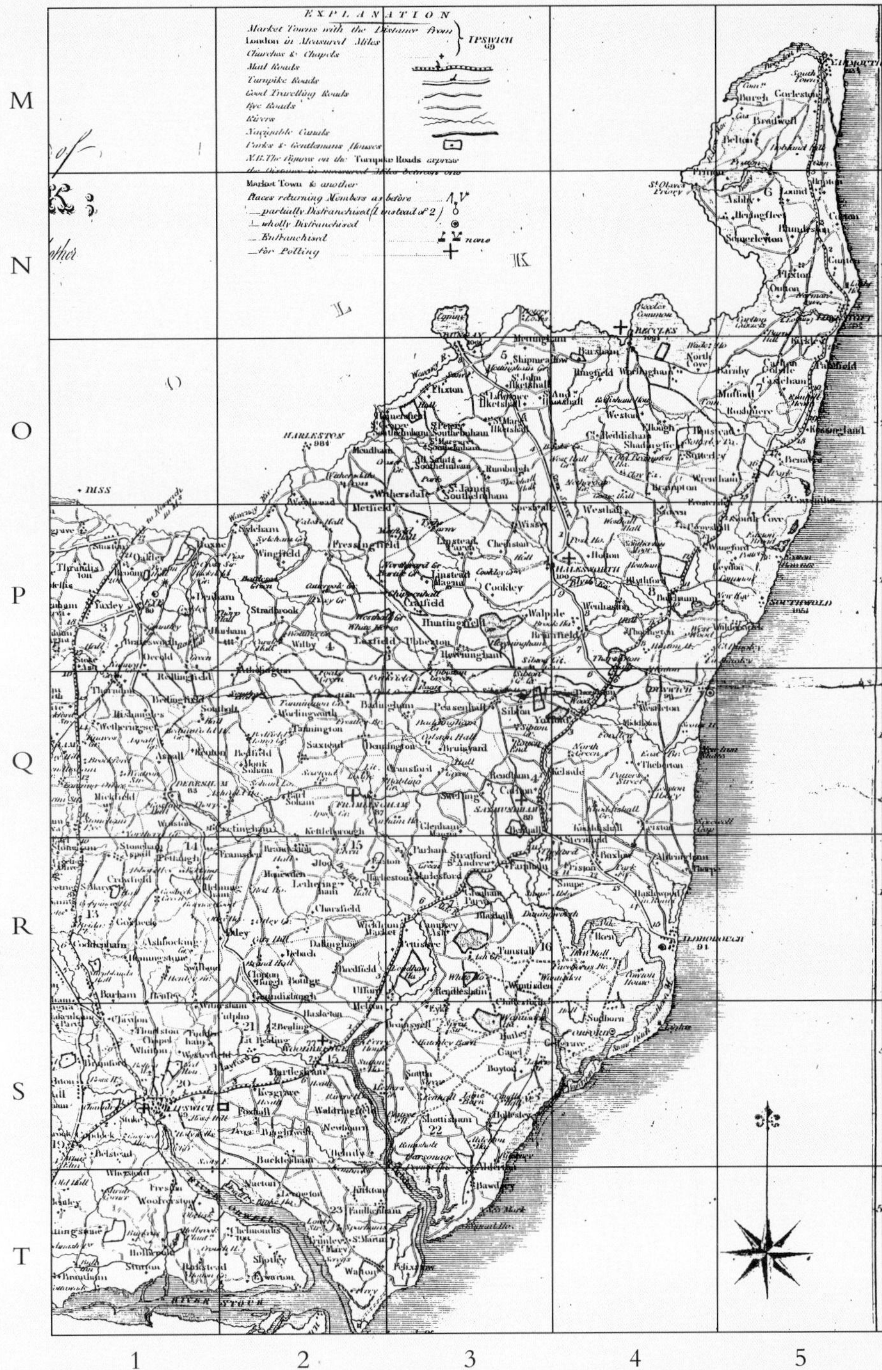

The Churchyard Children

All were taught to paint by their father and at least four became accomplished artists, Ellen, Laura, Anna and Harriet. The size of their respective output is indicated by the number of pictures they exhibited at the Ipswich Fine Arts Club following its inception in 1877: Anna 119, Laura 77, Harriet 26 and Ellen 7.

THOMAS *1825-1896*	Became a farmer and soon migrated to the colonies. No work by him has been identified.
ELLEN *1826-1909*	A skilled flower painter who rarely ventured into other subjects. Her prim meticulous style is quite distinct from her father's.
EMMA *1828-1878*	No work by her is known. She died comparatively young.
LAURA *1830-1891*	She and Anna were artistically closest to their father in that, like him, they were both prolific landscape painters. Laura, however, worked almost exclusively in watercolours. Her often elaborate themes are painted with great care but, though skillful in their way, they lack her father's fluid handling and inspired colour combinations. Generally regarded as the most gifted of the children.
ANNA *1832-1897*	More impulsive than Laura and tending towards the slapdash, she painted equally in oils and watercolour. While she is not thought capable of her father's refined and subtle elegance, it is nonetheless significant that so little of her extensive output is acknowledged today. It can only be concluded that, of all the children, she is the one whose work is most frequently mistaken for his.
ELIZABETH *1834-1913*	Usually known as Bessie. Comparatively unskilled and not a serious contender.
HARRIET *1836-1927*	An excellent artist specialising in portraits and genre subjects, frequently in a rural setting. She was also fond of contriving Punch-like joke pictures. Mainly worked in watercolour but, despite her long life, she was relatively unproductive. Is usually recognisable by her subject matter.
CATHERINE *1839-1888*	Known as Kate. Similar subjects to Harriet but lacking her ability. She only once exhibited at the Ipswich Fine Arts Club in 1879.
CHARLES *1841-1929*	Slightly more skilled than Bessie and Kate, but nonetheless a weak and conventional landscapist whose work is easily recognised. Known as Charley.

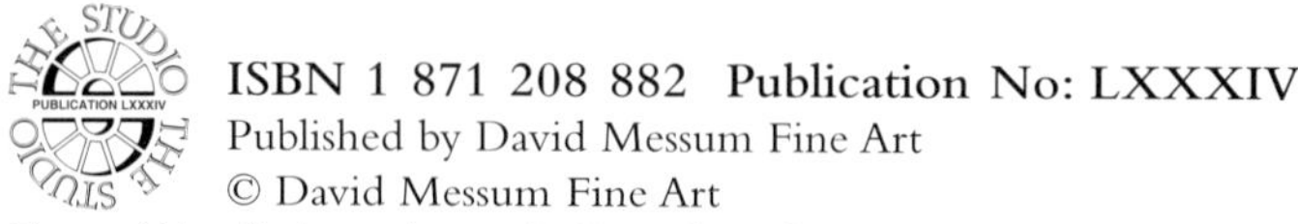

ISBN 1 871 208 882 Publication No: LXXXIV
Published by David Messum Fine Art

The Studio, Lords Wood, Marlow, Buckinghamshire. Tel: Marlow 01628 486565
Printed by Clarendon Printers Ltd., High Wycombe, Bucks.